MW01193659

American Rage

American Rage argues that anger is the central emotion governing contemporary US politics, with powerful, deleterious effects. Tracing the developments that have given rise to a culture of anger in the mass public, the book sheds new light on both public opinion and voting behavior. Steven W. Webster skillfully uses a combination of novel datasets, new measures of anger, and a series of experiments to show how anger causes citizens to lose trust in the national government and weakens their commitment to democratic norms and values. Despite these negative consequences, political elites strategically seek to elicit anger among their supporters. Presenting compelling evidence, Webster ultimately concludes that elites engage in this behavior because voter anger leads to voter loyalty. When voters are angry, they are more likely to vote for their party's slate of candidates at multiple levels of the federal electoral system.

Steven W. Webster is Assistant Professor of Political Science at Indiana University. His research interests include voter behavior, public opinion, and American elections.

American Rage

How Anger Shapes Our Politics

STEVEN W. WEBSTER

Indiana University

CAMBRIDGE
UNIVERSITY PRESS

University Printing House, Cambridge CB2 8BS, United Kingdom

One Liberty Plaza, 20th Floor, New York, NY 10006, USA

477 Williamstown Road, Port Melbourne, VIC 3207, Australia

314–321, 3rd Floor, Plot 3, Splendor Forum, Jasola District Centre,
New Delhi – 110025, India

79 Anson Road, #06–04/06, Singapore 079906

Cambridge University Press is part of the University of Cambridge.

It furthers the University's mission by disseminating knowledge in the pursuit of
education, learning, and research at the highest international levels of excellence.

www.cambridge.org
Information on this title: www.cambridge.org/9781108491372
DOI: 10.1017/9781108868303

© Steven W. Webster 2020

This publication is in copyright. Subject to statutory exception
and to the provisions of relevant collective licensing agreements,
no reproduction of any part may take place without the written
permission of Cambridge University Press.

First published 2020

A catalogue record for this publication is available from the British Library.

Library of Congress Cataloging-in-Publication Data
NAMES: Webster, Steven W., 1990– author.
TITLE: American rage : how anger shapes our politics / Steven W. Webster.
DESCRIPTION: Cambridge, United Kingdom ; New York, NY : Cambridge University
Press, 2020. | Includes bibliographical references and index.
IDENTIFIERS: LCCN 2020012948 (print) | LCCN 2020012949 (ebook) |
ISBN 9781108491372 (hardback) | ISBN 9781108811927 (paperback) |
ISBN 9781108868303 (epub)
SUBJECTS: LCSH: Political culture–United States. | Political psychology–United States. |
Anger–Political aspects–United States. | Voting research–United States. |
Party affiliation–United States. | United States–Politics and government–21st
century–Public opinion. | Public opinion–United States.
CLASSIFICATION: LCC JK1726 .W39 2020 (print) | LCC JK1726 (ebook) |
DDC 306.20973–dc23
LC record available at https://lccn.loc.gov/2020012948
LC ebook record available at https://lccn.loc.gov/2020012949

ISBN 978-1-108-49137-2 Hardback
ISBN 978-1-108-81192-7 Paperback

Cambridge University Press has no responsibility for the persistence or accuracy
of URLs for external or third-party internet websites referred to in this publication
and does not guarantee that any content on such websites is, or will remain,
accurate or appropriate.

For Wayne and Kathleen.

Contents

Figures

Tables

Preface

One of the most notable characteristics of American politics in the twenty-first century is the degree to which both Democrats and Republicans are angry at the opposing party, its leaders, and its supporters. In a January 2016 opinion piece for *The Washington Post*, Jennifer Rubin argued similarly, saying that "[a]nger has almost become a fad, a way of signaling that you know what's going on, you're sophisticated enough to see you're being taken advantage of."[1] Yet, if anger is a fad or the signal emotion of our day, the current body of scholarship knows far too little about the causes and political consequences of anger. Utilizing a combination of novel datasets, new measures of anger, and a series of experiments on people throughout the country, this book argues that anger is a powerful and all-present force in shaping patterns of political behavior and public opinion. Specifically, I argue that anger has served to reduce Americans' trust in their governing institutions, has weakened the citizenry's commitment to democratic norms and values, and has given rise to extraordinarily high levels of voter loyalty at multiple electoral levels.

Given such a holistic view of anger, this book is divided into two main parts. In the first part of the book, I give an overview of how anger affects American political behavior and public opinion. I also consider three primary developments that have given rise to the heightened levels of anger that currently exist in American politics. The first development that has given rise to anger is the sorting of partisan identities with racial,

---

[1] Rubin's piece can be found here: www.washingtonpost.com/blogs/right-turn/wp/2016/01/05/isnt-obama-responsible-for-some-of-this-anger/?utm_term=.dd8ac7224b54. Accessed June 4, 2018.

ethnic, cultural, and ideological identities. The increasing alignment of these crucial identities has led to a society where the demarcations between "us" and "them" have grown ever clearer. These divisions, in turn, have helped to create and perpetuate an anger-fueled style of politics.

The second development that has contributed to the growth in anger is the development of what Prior (2007) has labeled the "post-broadcast" media environment. Characterized by explicitly partisan and ideological news outlets, this new media landscape has allowed Democrats and Republicans to self-select into news outlets that do little more than confirm their preexisting beliefs and further entrench their partisan identities. The third – and related – development that has helped to fuel the growth in anger is the emergence of the Internet and associated technologies that serve to exacerbate partisan divisions. How these three trends have led to the creation of an increasingly angry electorate is the subject of Chapter 1.

After outlining an argument as to how partisan sorting has led to an anger-fueled style of politics, I finish the first part of the book by showing in Chapter 2 that political elites actively seek to elicit anger among the electorate. Utilizing the universe of tweets sent by presidential candidates during the 2016 campaign, as well as the transcripts of broadcast TV shows that aired on Fox News and MSNBC between 1999 and 2016, I show that political elites do seek to elicit anger among their supporters. Additionally, I present evidence that suggests that political elites are more likely to elicit this anger during key points of a campaign.

In the second part of the book, comprising Chapters 3 through 6, I illustrate the ways in which anger shapes patterns of public opinion and voter behavior. In Chapter 3 I introduce a measure of trait-based anger, derived from clinical psychology, to show how an individual's predisposition to be angry shapes their evaluations of the national government across two different metrics. Moreover, I show how the relationship between personality-governed levels of anger and evaluations of the national government is moderated by partisan affiliation.

Chapter 4 moves beyond studying anger as a personality trait and examines the relationship between anger, conceptualized as an emotion, and trust in government. To do so, I utilize an experimental design that allows me to determine the causal effect of heightened levels of anger on trust in government. The experimental design randomizes individuals into one of three different treatment conditions: a condition that primes apolitical anger, a condition that elicits anger specifically about politics, or a condition that increases the salience of politics or political issues. This design feature is important because it both facilitates an experiment with clearly defined interventions and allows for a straightforward examination of possible heterogeneous treatment effects. The results suggest that both apolitical anger and targeted political anger lower citizens' trust in the national government. In fact, the effect of apolitical anger on lowering trust in government is just as strong as the effect of political anger. This suggests that the *magnitude*, and not necessarily the *source*, is the most important element in anger's ability to weaken the bonds of trust between Americans and their governing institutions.

In Chapter 5, I examine the role of anger in weakening citizens' commitment to democratic norms and values. Utilizing a similar experimental design to the one employed in Chapter 4, this chapter examines the causal effect of anger on Americans' support for political tolerance, respect for minority opinions, and a commitment to maintaining "the spirit of the law" in addition to "the letter of the law." The results suggest that higher levels of anger serve to reduce Americans' commitment to these essential norms and values – particularly with respect to political tolerance – that have long been the lynchpin of a well-functioning democratic society.

The results I present in this book yield a puzzling question: If anger has a harmful effect on American government and politics, then why do political elites persist in seeking to provoke anger among their followers? Chapter 6 argues that political elites seek to elicit anger among their followers because voter anger leads to voter loyalty. In this chapter I show that more frequently feeling angry toward the opposing party's presidential candidate is predictive of higher levels of voter loyalty. This relationship is most pronounced for those individuals who do not particularly like their own party's presidential candidate. Among this subgroup of the electorate, higher degrees of anger leads to behavior more characteristic of committed partisans. Additionally, the evidence presented in this chapter suggests that, in the current era of nationalized politics, anger toward the opposing party's presidential candidate leads to voter loyalty in subpresidential elections.

Finally, I conclude with a chapter discussing anger and the future of American government and politics. Is it possible to reverse the rise of anger within the electorate, or is this contentious style of politics here to stay? The answer has lasting implications for public opinion, political behavior, and the nature of political competition in the United States.

Acknowledgments

This book would not have been possible without the generous assistance of so many people. Alan Abramowitz has been a consistent supporter of this work, a true friend, and a real source of encouragement throughout this project. The book itself likely would have never come to fruition if it weren't for Adam Glynn, whose gentle nudging over lunch one day convinced me that writing a book was work worth doing. His belief in my research, as well as his willingness to offer advice when I was stuck, have both been invaluable. Andrew Reeves and Betsy Sinclair both deserve a tremendous amount of thanks as well. Andrew was instrumental in the progression of this manuscript and never hesitated to read through drafts of chapters. Betsy's enthusiasm, encouragement, and belief gave me the motivation to finish this manuscript. Thanks are also due to Chris Lucas, who has been a sounding board for my ideas and a consistent source of optimism.

I am also grateful for having had the opportunity to work with such a wonderful group of people at Cambridge University Press. At every stage of the publication process, the team at Cambridge has been top-notch. My editor, Sara Doskow, expressed an early interest in my ideas and has done much to shepherd this project through to completion. Additionally, I am thankful to the anonymous reviewers of this manuscript. Their detailed comments and suggestions have done much to strengthen the manuscript.

Finally, I must thank my family for their support throughout the writing process. This book would not have been possible without any of them.

However, special thanks are due to Melanie Gomez, whose phone calls were both a source of levity and a way to stay up to date with political current events as I was finishing this manuscript. Thanks, as well, to my grandparents, whose dedication to their country and their commitment to the political process were unrivaled. This book is dedicated to their memory.

The Rise of Anger in the American Public

It's quick, it's binary, it's delicious. And more and more, we're gorging on it.
— Time Magazine, on anger, June 2016[1]

The 2016 presidential election in the United States laid bare a reality about the country's political scene: Americans are angry. Presented with two candidates who were both historically unpopular, the level of vitriol and disgust exhibited by both sides of the political divide was noteworthy. Yet, while the 2016 election was characterized by these notably high levels of anger, such negativity was not a sudden development. In fact, the anger-fueled election of Donald Trump to the presidency was part of a trend that had been developing for decades.

Indeed, politicians have long known that anger can be a useful tactic for furthering their electoral goals. For example, during his successful campaign for Congress in 1978, Newt Gingrich spoke to a group of College Republicans about what he saw as the fundamental difference between the Democratic and Republican parties. The Democrats, Gingrich argued, "always produced young, nasty people who had no respect for their elders." By contrast, the Republicans encouraged their supporters to be "neat, obedient, and loyal and faithful and all those Boy Scout words, which would be great around the camp fire, but are lousy in politics." The solution to the Republicans' woes, according to Gingrich, was to encourage their supporters "to be nasty." To drive home his point,

---

[1] Quote taken from Kluger (2016). The entire article can be read at http://time.com/4353606/anger-america-enough-already/.

Gingrich urged his audience to "stand up ...in a slug fest and match it out with their opponent[s]."[2]

Gingrich's wish for a zero-sum, winner-take-all, anger-fueled style of politics has been aided by the dramatic growth of "negative partisanship," which Alan Abramowitz and I have developed in a series of articles (Abramowitz and Webster 2016, 2018*b*). A phenomenon describing the ways in which Americans' political behavior is more often guided by the candidates and parties they *dislike* rather than the ones they *like*, negative partisanship "is flipping politics on its head" as "voters form strong loyalties based more on loathing for the opposing party than on the old kind of tribal loyalty" seen in previous eras (Fournier 2015; Zahn 2016). As a chief component of negative partisanship, the central argument of this book is that anger has the profound ability to alter American political behavior and public opinion. Moreover, anger is not synonymous with partisan or ideological polarization. Though it is conceptually related to polarization – and most salient for guiding political behavior when polarization is high – anger has consequences that move beyond polarization-induced congressional gridlock (Binder 1999, 2004; Krehbiel 1998), altered legislative agendas (Cox and McCubbins 2005), or "unorthodox" styles of lawmaking (Sinclair 1997). Indeed, anger has deeply affected American political behavior and public opinion in three distinct ways: it has lowered Americans' trust in the national government, it has caused Americans to weaken in their commitment to democratic norms and values, and it has produced extraordinarily high levels of partisan loyalty at the ballot box.

In this chapter, I begin by conceptualizing anger: what it is, how it arises, and what its effects are. I then discuss the psychological mechanisms behind anger's ability to affect political behavior and public opinion in contemporary American politics. Next, I discuss three important ways in which anger shapes public opinion and political behavior. The first way in which anger affects public opinion and political behavior is by lowering citizens' trust in their government. Given its necessity in "making Washington work" (Hetherington and Rudolph 2015), understanding the historical trend in citizens' trust in government – as well as some potential reasons for its precipitous decline – is of paramount importance. I also argue that anger affects public opinion and political behavior by weakening citizens' commitment to democratic norms, those

---

[2] Gingrich's remarks to the College Republicans can be found in full at www.pbs.org/wgbh/pages/frontline/newt/newt78speech.html.

sorts of "informal institutions" (Helmke and Levitsky 2006; Lauth 2000) that dictate which types of behavior are proprietous and which are not. Finally, I argue that anger is crucial in forging partisan loyalty. In this sense, the growth in anger within the American electorate has reshaped political behavior by increasing partisan loyalty and decreasing citizens' affective evaluations of the opposing political party. Finally, I conclude by discussing the relationship between anger and negative partisanship with a focus on the trends that have helped to create and sustain the current climate of anger-fueled negative partisanship in American politics.

1.1 WHAT IS ANGER?

Anger, like happiness, or anxiety, or fear, is both a personality trait and an emotion. What, then, are personality traits and emotions? Personality traits are "internally based psychological characteristics" (Allen 1994) that define "who we are as individuals" (Mondak 2010). Personality traits are the psychological forces behind individual differences in behavior, tastes, and thoughts (Wiggins 1996). Accordingly, personality traits shape the ways in which different individuals respond to the same situation. These different situational responses arise due to the varying degrees to which individuals possess various personality traits and encounter particular stimuli. As Buss (1999) notes, "all individuals may possess a psychological mechanism of jealousy, but differ in the degree to which they enduringly occupy an environment filled with threats to their ... relationships." Personality traits, then, are deep-seated phenotypic characteristics of an individual that guide patterns of behavior and tend to remain stable throughout the course of the lifespan (Allen 1994; McCrae and Costa 1994).

Emotions, by contrast, are more ephemeral and can best be thought of as momentary feelings. Indeed, according to James's (1884) classic analysis of the subject, an "emotion" is simply a feeling that corresponds to various actions and bodily stimuli. For others, such as LeDoux (1998), emotions are distinctly "biological functions of the nervous system." Emotions are usually, though not always, aroused in response to some event and fade with time. Accordingly, a key difference between emotions and personality traits is that the former are manipulatable, while the latter are not. That emotions are manipulatable plays a crucial role in much of the analyses in this book, particularly in Chapters 4 and 5.

Regardless of whether it is studied as a personality trait (as in Chapter 3) or an emotion (as in Chapters 4 and 5), there are key features that differentiate anger from other emotions or personality traits. The first differentiator is that anger is negatively valenced (Lerner and Tiedens 2006; Moons, Eisenberger, and Taylor 2010). Put simply, anger is something that is felt when one is irritated, frustrated, upset, or begrudged. This contrasts with happiness, joy, or contentment, all of which are positively valenced. A second aspect that is unique to anger is that it often causes individuals to attribute blame to a specific person, group of people, or entity. Moreover, anger causes people to seek some form of retribution toward that which elicited their anger (Allred 1999; Allred et al. 1997; Bower 1991). A third differentiator between anger and other emotions is that anger typically causes individuals to "mentally retreat." In other words, anger causes people to both fall back on the information and beliefs that they already have and increase their reliance on group-based cues or heuristics (Bodenhausen, Sheppard, and Kramer 1994). These reactions differ from those engendered by anxiety, for example, which has been shown to push individuals to seek new information (see, e.g., Albertson and Gadarian 2015). These characteristics of anger – its negative valence; the fact that it often leads to an attribution of blame and the search for retribution; and its ability to cause individuals to rely on what they already know, and to increase their reliance on group-based heuristics – will be key theoretical elements in the chapters to come. Next, I briefly outline the ways in which these three characteristics of anger affect patterns of political behavior and public opinion.

1.2 ANGER, PUBLIC OPINION, AND MASS POLITICAL BEHAVIOR

Traditional models of political behavior often assume that Americans' political choices are governed by rational decision making (Downs 1957), sincere ideological policy preferences (Abramowitz 2010), or through group-based notions of partisan identification (Green, Palmquist, and Schickler 2002; Mason 2015). Though these are important mechanisms for guiding political behavior and public opinion, Americans form opinions about political institutions, adopt attitudes about democratic governance, and make choices at the ballot box for more psychologically rooted reasons (Marcus 2002; Marcus, Neuman, and MacKuen 2000). Indeed, an individual's felt emotions (Banks 2014) and personality profile (Gerber et al. 2010; Johnston, Federico, and Lavine 2017) have both been shown to affect political behavior in profound ways. In the current era of American politics, which is characterized by high levels of animosity between partisans, anger is likely to be among the most powerful of emotions and personality traits shaping the ways in which Americans interact with the political system.

One way in which anger affects public opinion and political behavior is through its negative valence. All emotions have either a positive or a negative valence, and the direction of this valence is important in determining how individuals both perceive and react to that which aroused the emotion in the first place (Bower 1991). Emotions with a positive valence, such as happiness or joy, will cause people to evaluate other people, places, and ideas in a positive light. Emotions with a negative valence, such as anger, will lead people to evaluate those same people, places, or ideas in a negative fashion (Moons, Eisenberger, and Taylor 2010; Schwarz and Clore 1983). Thus, when individuals are made angry by politics, politicians, or political affairs, their felt emotion will push them to render negative evaluations of those politicians or political affairs that elicited their anger (see, for instance, Bennett 1997; Lerner and Tiedens 2006).

Yet, anger need not be elicited specifically by politics or some political actor in order to shape Americans' views of the political world. In fact, it is possible for generalized apolitical anger, or "incidental anger," to also affect Americans' political behavior and opinions. That incidental anger can affect political views stems from the fact that emotions are not easily compartmentalized. In fact, anger in one setting can – and often does – spill over into completely different settings (Dunn and Schweitzer 2005). Moreover, anger aroused in one aspect of an individual's life can alter evaluations of objects completely orthogonal to the person or stimulus that initially aroused their anger (Forgas and Moylan 1987). As a result, anger – whether targeted political anger or generalized apolitical anger – is capable of shaping patterns of political behavior and public opinion. In this book, I draw on these properties to show how individuals who are angry – whether specifically about politics or something apolitical – have lower evaluations of the national government.

Anger also affects political behavior through its tendency to cause people to blame others for perceived wrongdoings and, moreover, to seek retribution for that which elicited the anger (Allred 1999; Weiner 2000). Survey data suggests that Democrats and Republicans today are increasingly angry at each other and are likely to attribute blame for the country's ills to the opposing political party and its supporters.[3]

---

[3] This claim is derived from a report by the Pew Research Center, "Partisanship and Political Animosity in 2016," which highlights the growing animosity between Democrats and Republicans in the American electorate. The report can be found here: www.people-press.org/2016/06/22/partisanship-and-political-animosity-in-2016/.

Such anger-fueled blame has the potential to lead Democrats (Republicans) toward the action of lowering evaluations of Republicans (Democrats) *as people* by doubting the legitimacy of their opinions and their personal intelligence. In this sense, anger can weaken Americans' commitment to democratic norms and values such as political tolerance and the respect for minority rights.

Finally, anger can affect political behavior by causing individuals to "mentally retreat" by increasing their reliance on group-based cues and heuristics. In the context of American politics, no group-based cue or heuristic is stronger or more prevalent than partisan identification (Campbell et al. 1960). Accordingly, when Americans are made angry, they are likely to increase their reliance on their identity *as partisans*. This increased focus on partisan identities, in turn, has the ability to increase voters' loyalty to their party's slate of candidates at all electoral levels.

1.3 TRENDS IN PUBLIC OPINION AND POLITICAL BEHAVIOR

Recent years have seen the emergence of three distinct patterns or trends in public opinion and political behavior. First, Americans are exhibiting lower levels of trust in their government. Second, Americans appear to be less committed to democratic norms and values. Third, and finally, Americans are increasingly voting loyally for their own political party's slate of candidates even though they are professing to be politically independent (see, e.g., Klar and Krupnikov 2016).

The primary argument of this book is that anger, as described above, has caused and helped to perpetuate these three trends. That is, anger has facilitated a decline in citizens' trust in their own government, has weakened Americans' commitment to democratic norms and values, and has forged partisan loyalty at various levels of electoral competition. In this section, I briefly describe these three trends. Later chapters will more explicitly detail how and why anger affects trust in government, commitment to democratic norms, and partisan loyalty in voting behavior.

1.3.1 Declining Trust in Government

Since the Dwight Eisenhower era, Americans have become increasingly distrustful of their government. Figure 1.1 plots the moving average of the

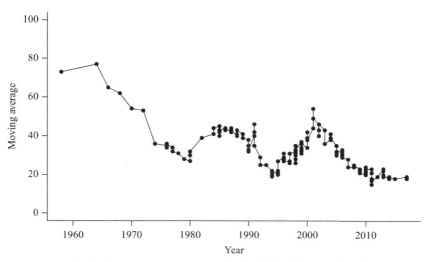

FIGURE 1.1. Declining trust in government in the United States. This figure shows the extent to which Americans have come to distrust their government over time. The line indicates the moving average of the percentage of Americans who say they trust the government "always" or "most of the time." Data comes from the CBS/NY Times Poll, the ABC/Washington Post Poll, Gallup, Pew Research Center, and the American National Election Studies.

percentage of Americans who say they trust the government "always" or "most of the time." As can be seen, the apex of Americans' trust in their government was at the beginning of the time series. Over the past fifty-five years, the percentage of Americans who say they trust the government has fallen precipitously.[4] By 2015, only 20% of Americans said they trust the government.

This sharp decline in the percentage of Americans who say they trust the government is problematic for multiple reasons. As Hetherington and Rudolph (2015) note, trust in government can facilitate bipartisan legislation and compromise. Absent trust in the institution of government, gridlock and partisan grandstanding is likely to persist. Yet, more important than its ability to induce bipartisan legislation is trust's role in facilitating support for government programs that benefit the most disadvantaged members of society. As Hetherington (2005) argues, "people need to trust

---

4 One notable upward spike in Americans' trust in government occurred shortly after the September 11, 2001, terrorist attacks.

the government when they pay the costs but do not receive the benefits" of social welfare programs. Otherwise, support for such programs will diminish and collective outcomes will be suboptimal. Trust, according to Hetherington (2005), is essential to societal and political prosperity.

Moreover, this secular decline in trust in government is problematic because trust is a necessary component of governmental legitimacy. Democratic theory argues that the people are sovereign and that they should have a say – directly or, as in the case of the United States, indirectly – in governmental decision making. Absent trust in the very organization that is meant to aggregate and represent individuals' interests, it is hard to imagine a functioning and robust democracy.

If trust is essential to the democratic process, what, then, is causing Americans to lose trust in the government? Hetherington and Rudolph (2015), building on earlier work by Citrin (1974), suggest that Americans' trust in government is a function of their partisanship. More specifically, this line of thought argues that Americans trust the government when their own political party holds power. Conversely, when the opposing party is in charge, Americans have lower trust in the government. While partisanship certainly plays a role, this theoretical argument is difficult to square with the trends shown in Figure 1.1. Indeed, if trust in government was purely a function of partisanship, it is not clear why we should see the downward trends that we do, in fact, observe. If partisanship was the sole reason Americans gained or lost trust in government, the over-time trend in trust in government should be characterized by slight perturbations around some mean level of trust as party control of the government switches back and forth. That we see a continual decline suggests something else is happening – something which cuts across partisanship.

One of the arguments that I make in this book is that the rise of anger in American politics has been an important and overlooked reason that Americans have lost trust in their government. In Chapter 3, I show how higher levels of trait-based anger are associated with lower levels of trust in the government across a variety of metrics. I also show how this relationship is moderated by an individual's partisan affiliation. In Chapter 4, I utilize a survey experiment on a national sample of registered American voters to show that anger – both political and apolitical in nature – has a causal effect on reducing trust in government.

1.3.2 Weakening Commitment to Democratic Norms

In addition to being noteworthy for dangerously low levels of trust in government, American politics today is more adversarial and less tolerant of opposition points of view than in previous years. This rancorous political competition is the result of Americans' increasing willingness to flaunt long-held democratic norms that dictate the ways in which politics should be approached. To the extent that democracy is, as Bernard Shaw said, "a device that ensures we shall be governed no better than we deserve," then the nature of contemporary American political behavior is worrisome.

As Levitsky and Ziblatt (2018) note in their analysis of "how democracies die," democratic governance is not something that is protected merely by a codification of rules, regulations, and institutional arrangements within a constitutional framework. While such a written commitment to democracy as "the only game in town" is important to democratic health, Levitsky and Ziblatt (2018) note that democracy is best served when these codified rules of the game "are reinforced by norms of mutual toleration and restraint in the exercise of power." That these norms have begun to disappear has been a chief characteristic of modern-day American political competition.

A recent Pew Research Center report sheds light on Americans' gradual disregard for democratic norms. According to the Pew report, a growing percentage of Americans no longer view supporters of the opposing political party as merely those who hold a different political opinion than themselves. Instead, a large percentage of both Democrats (41%) and Republicans (45%) see the policies advocated by the other party as a threat to the country. Moreover, the Pew report notes that both Democrats and Republicans are likely to believe that the political views one holds says "a lot" about the kind of person they are. Indeed, 63% of Republicans agreed that how a person thinks about politics says a lot about the kind of person they are, while 70% of Democrats felt similarly.[5]

This increasing willingness to view supporters of the other party as dangerous and to view the totality of an individual in terms of their political beliefs has potentially catastrophic consequences. In fact, recent

---

[5] The report, "Partisanship and Political Animosity in 2016," can be found in full at www.people-press.org/2016/06/22/partisanship-and-political-animosity-in-2016/. Accessed May 19, 2018.

work suggests that this extreme dislike and lack of tolerance for those who hold different political opinions has the potential to spill over into support for physical violence. Utilizing a series of experiments surrounding the 2016 presidential election, Kalmoe (2018) found that partisans were more supportive of state-sponsored violence toward out-party supporters than toward their fellow partisans when these individuals were engaging in civic protest. Notably, such support for violence "is not limited to extremists – it resides comfortably in the attitudes and behaviors of ordinary partisans when legitimized and mobilized by the state." This support for violence can also affect how partisans view in-party members who are not sufficiently ideologically extreme. Indeed, new work suggests that some partisans wish ill-health or even death on those party members who do not support the party's agenda.[6]

This extreme dislike – dislike to the degree of wishing physical violence or some other harm on those who hold different political views – is deleterious to the proper functioning of democratic government. As Svolik (2018) cogently shows, heightened political polarization within a society can push citizens to put their partisan interests over the country's well-being. More specifically, Svolik's (2018) work illustrates how authoritarian leaders can subvert democratic processes by exploiting the fact that polarized societies often produce a situation in which partisans' dislike of the opposing political party outweighs their concern for free and fair elections. Thus, Svolik (2018) concludes that "electoral competition often confronts voters with a choice between democratic values and partisan interests, and ...a significant fraction of a polarized electorate may be willing to sacrifice the former in favor of the latter."

The dramatic growth in negative partisanship and affective polarization within the electorate, which I will highlight in Section 1.4, indicates that the United States is in a perilous position in terms of the respect for democratic norms. Heightened partisan antipathy in the country has led to a scenario where citizens wish ill-will on those on the other side of the political divide, as Kalmoe (2018) has found, and has produced an environment where the country is vulnerable to the democracy-versus-partisanship tradeoff described by Svolik (2018). In Chapter 5, I build on these studies by showing how higher levels of anger have a causal effect

---

[6] See this report in *The Washington Post* "Monkey Cage" section: www.washingtonpost .com/news/monkey-cage/wp/2018/05/16/surprised-by-the-anger-toward-mccain-party-loyalists-can-hate-apostates-as-much-as-opponents/. Accessed May 21, 2018.

on lowering citizens' support for a series of democratic norms that have long governed American political competition.

1.3.3 High Partisan Loyalty

In addition to declining trust in government and a weakening commitment to democratic norms, the contemporary American political era is characterized by a high degree of partisan loyalty in voting behavior. While previous decades saw Americans vote for a candidate of one party for president and a candidate of the other party at subpresidential levels, the nature of modern-day political competition is noteworthy for its high degree of straight-ticket voting. This trend implies that the advantage often enjoyed by incumbents has been declining in favor of a more partisan style of representation.

This "atrophy of the incumbency advantage" was cogently articulated by Jacobson (2015), who utilized a combination of aggregate-level election data and survey data to show that incumbent politicians are receiving the lowest vote shares since the 1950s. According to his study, incumbency for members of the House of Representatives is worth less than 4 percentage points. Jacobson (2015) further notes that this decline in the incumbency advantage in favor of high partisan loyalty has disproportionately affected the electoral fortunes of Democratic candidates. This is because, while Republicans in the electorate are spread thinly across electoral districts, Democratic partisans tend to cluster in urban areas. Thus, there are more "wasted votes" for Democratic candidates than Republican candidates (see also, Abramowitz and Webster 2016).

The decline in the incumbency advantage in lieu of high partisan loyalty has potential problems for democratic governance and representation. Earlier years saw politicians develop a particular "homestyle" that aided their overarching goal of re-election (Fenno 1978; Mayhew 1974). This "homestyle" entailed the courting of votes by a politician pointing out the ways in which he or she had successfully obtained federal monies or projects for his or her district. In this way, campaigns were motivated by a desire to illustrate one's efficacy in constituency service and representation while in office. Importantly, such constituent service cut across party lines. As a result, re-election was often achieved by personal contact and a high degree of name recognition.

With the rise of high partisan loyalty in voting behavior, the incentives for politicians to govern and campaign in such a bipartisan fashion have been removed. Instead of appealing to constituents across party lines, politicians in the contemporary era are largely focused on appealing to their own party's supporters while ignoring the desires of the opposing party's supporters. Rather than trumpeting their bipartisan bona fides and focusing on bringing federal funds back to their district, contemporary politicians are most concerned with signaling their commitment to the partisan cause and representing constituents on national issues (Lapinski et al. 2016). The end result of these changes has been a reorientation of constituent representation; rather than representing all of their constituents, politicians today are concerned only with representing those constituents who belong to the same political party as themselves.

In Chapter 6, I argue that the growth in anger in the American electorate has been an important reason that contemporary elections are characterized by such a high degree of partisan loyalty. When individuals are made to be angry at the opposing political party and its candidates, the costs of failing to vote for one's own party's candidates – and, as a result, perhaps being represented by the opposing party – are too high. I also show that this relationship is not merely a byproduct of elite-level polarization. Simply put, an angry voter is a loyal voter, and the existence of anger is not dependent upon polarization.

1.4 RAGE, NEGATIVE PARTISANSHIP, AND THE SOURCES OF ANGER

Anger, whether experienced habitually due to personality traits or aroused emotionally, has the potential to alter the ways in which Americans engage with the political world. While Americans in previous eras used to feel indifferent toward the opposing political party and its supporters, the contemporary era is one in which Democrats loathe Republicans and Republicans abhor Democrats. This mutual dislike between partisans has led to a new style of political competition, one in which partisan loyalty is achieved by engendering anger toward the opposing party. Such anger has been growing over time.

This rising antipathy manifests itself most clearly when examining the trends in partisans' affective evaluations of both their own party and the opposing party. Beginning in 1978, the American National Election Studies (ANES) began asking respondents to rate both of the two major political parties on a "feeling thermometer" scale. This measure ranges

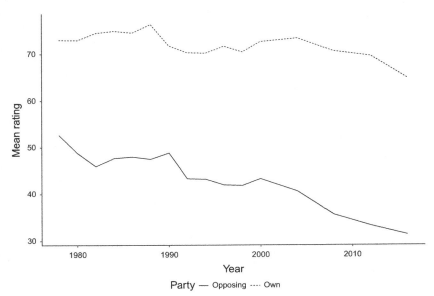

FIGURE 1.2. The growth of negative partisan affect. This figure shows the mean ratings Americans have given to their own and the opposing political party over the past thirty-eight years.

from 0 to 100, with zero indicating the worst possible rating and 100 the best. Since this question was first asked, Americans' affective evaluations of their own political party have changed very little. Indeed, the mean rating that individuals gave their own party between 1978 and 2012 changed by only 3.4 points. Though partisans exhibited more negative feelings toward their own party in 2016, the overall trend shows only a minimal degree of movement.[7]

The most drastic change over this thirty-eight-year time span has been in the affective ratings that Americans have given the opposing party. In 1978, Americans largely felt neutral toward the out-party. In fact, the mean rating given to the opposing party was 52.6 – about as neutral as can be. However, there has been a nearly monotonic decrease in affective ratings of the opposing party ever since. By 2016, Americans' ratings of the opposing political party on the feeling thermometer scale had fallen to 31.3. These trends are shown in Figure 1.2.

---

7 These numbers, as well as the following numbers in this chapter, are calculated using the face-to-face weights in the ANES cumulative file.

This trend toward partisan negativity, referred to by some as "negative partisanship" (Abramowitz and Webster 2016, 2018*b*) and others as "affective polarization" (Iyengar, Sood, and Lelkes 2012; Rogowski and Sutherland 2015), appears in more than just Americans' ratings of the two political parties. In fact, this negative partisan affect has spilled over to views toward the opposing party's presidential candidates. Between 1980 and 2012, the average rating of the opposing party's presidential candidate on the feeling thermometer scale dropped from 46.6 to 31.8 degrees. In 2016, the presence of Donald Trump and Hillary Clinton – two highly unpopular presidential candidates – pushed the mean rating of the opposing party's presidential candidate down to 19 degrees.

These negative views toward the opposing party's presidential candidates have oftentimes translated into anger directed at the candidate. Though not uniformly so, since the 1980s there has been an increase in the percentage of respondents to the ANES surveys who have indicated that they felt angry at the opposing party's presidential candidate. In 1980, just under 50% of respondents to the ANES surveys reported ever feeling angry at the opposing party's presidential candidate. By 2012, that percentage had jumped to 65%. By 2016, that number had reached an even higher mark, soaring to an astonishing 90%.

The rise of the anger-fueled nature of negative partisanship in contemporary American politics likely has many causes. However, three factors appear to be particularly important. The first factor has been the rise of partisan sorting, wherein partisan identities have become closely aligned with racial, cultural, and ideological identities. The second factor has been the advent of the "post-broadcast" media environment characterized by news outlets that offer ideologically friendly viewpoints (Prior 2007). Finally, the rapid technological growth in the twenty-first century and the increasing relevance of Internet-based news outlets has also helped to perpetuate the primacy of anger in modern American politics. Indeed, these second and third factors – the development of a new media environment and the growth of the Internet and related technologies – have made it easier for political elites to strategically elicit anger by capitalizing on the partisan alignment of racial, cultural, and ideological identities.

1.4.1 Partisan Sorting

Along racial, ethnic, cultural, and ideological dimensions, the contemporary Democratic and Republican parties look dramatically different than their mid-twentieth-century counterparts. Once a heterogeneous collection of people, the two major political parties have become internally homogeneous and externally distinct. This process, which has resulted in the alignment of partisan identities with racial, ethnic, cultural, and ideological identities, is known as partisan sorting (Bafumi and Shapiro 2009; Levendusky 2009; Mason 2015). With the bases of support for the Democratic and Republican parties so distinct along a multitude of dimensions, it has become easy for supporters of one party to see members of the opposing party as "the other." This has led to the rise of negative partisanship (Abramowitz and Webster 2016, 2018b), affective polarization (Iyengar, Sood, and Lelkes 2012; Rogowski and Sutherland 2015), and a culture of anger in today's politics.

Perhaps the most drastic change has been in the racial and ethnic composition of the two major parties. According to data from the ANES, in the 1952 election both of the parties were largely White. Indeed, 95% of Republicans were White as were 90% of Democrats. By 2016 the share of White Democrats had dropped to 57%, while Whites remained a much higher share of the Republican Party (83%). The drop in the percentage of White Democrats saw a concomitant increase in the percentage of Black and Hispanic supporters. By the turn of the millennium, the average percentage of Democrats who were Black was just under 20%. During this same time period, the average percentage of Democrats who were Hispanic was just under 10%. For Republicans, these same figures were 2.3% and 7.3%, respectively. The complete trend in the non-White share of each of the two parties is plotted in Figure 1.3.

The reasons for this racial and ethnic sorting are numerous, though its roots lie in the Democrats' support for civil rights legislation over the opposition of White Southerners. This support led White Southerners, who had been the bulwark of the "Solid South," to abandon the Democrats and utilize the Republican Party as their vehicle of racial conservatism (Hood, Kidd, and Morris 2004). The passage of the Civil Rights Act of 1964 and the Voting Rights Act of 1965 were watershed moments in national politics that, according to Black and Black (2002), "reformed southern race relations and helped destabilize the traditional one-party system." The racial coalitions of the Democrats and Republicans would never again be the same.

In addition to this change in the racial and ethnic composition of the two parties, Democrats and Republicans in the electorate are increasingly divided on cultural issues. To illustrate the degree of partisan sorting in terms of cultural issues over the past thirty years, consider the divergent

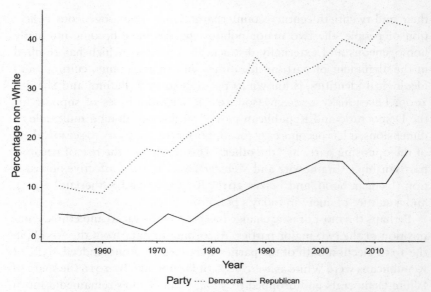

FIGURE 1.3. Change in racial composition of the parties. This figure shows the trend in the percentage of non-White individuals in each of the two parties.

partisan trends in terms of moral traditionalism. This scale, introduced to the ANES in 1986, is comprised of four questions that seek to measure the degree to which an individual prioritizes traditional morality and cultural views vis-à-vis moral liberalism. Each question asks individuals to indicate their level of disagreement or agreement with the following statements:

- Newer lifestyles are contributing to the breakdown of our society.
- The world is always changing and we should adjust our view of moral behavior to those changes.
- This country would have many fewer problems if there were more emphasis on traditional family ties.
- We should be more tolerant of people who choose to live according to their own moral standards, even if they are very different from our own.

Possible responses to these statements are "agree strongly," "agree somewhat," "neither agree nor disagree," "disagree somewhat," and "disagree strongly."[8] Responses to each statement are coded on a 0–4 scale, where higher values indicate higher levels of moral traditionalism. An individual's total score on the moral traditionalism scale is obtained by summing the scores for each of the composite items. The scale ranges from 0 to 16.

The trends in the mean level of moral traditionalism by partisan affiliation are staggering. In 1986, when the ANES first asked this battery of questions, the mean score on the moral traditionalism scale among Republicans was 10.1. The mean score for Democrats was a slightly smaller 9.38, providing a partisan differential of 0.72 points. By 2016, the mean score on the moral traditionalism scale for Republican respondents had fallen slightly to 9.95, while Democrats' mean score dropped to an all-time low of 6.34. Though Republicans' mean score on this measure had reached its apex in the mid-1990s before gradually falling, the partisan gap in 2016 (3.61) was the largest on record since the ANES began tracking views on moral traditionalism.

Perhaps more important than the mean scores on the moral traditionalism measure is the precise nature of the intraparty changes. To more precisely illustrate the partisan differences in terms of moral traditionalism I split the scale into quartiles. Figure 1.4 displays the percentage of Democrats and Republicans scoring in each of the quartiles by year. What is most noteworthy about the trends displayed in this figure is that the majority of the changes have occurred in the first and fourth quartiles. Indeed, between 1986 and 2016, the percentage of Democrats scoring in the first quartile on the moral traditionalism scale has increased by 69.1%. Meanwhile, the percentage of Democrats scoring in the fourth quartile on the moral traditionalism scale has dropped 69.2% over this same time period. The trend among Republicans over these thirty years has been just the opposite: the percentage of Republicans scoring in the fourth quartile has increased by 38.5% while the percentage of Republicans scoring in the first quartile has decreased by 30.1%.

Equally illuminating are the trends in the second and third quartiles. The change in the percentage of Democrats and Republican scoring in these quartiles has been comparatively less dramatic. Over the thirty-year span, only 6% fewer Democrats score in the second quartile; among Republicans there has been a 11.5% decrease in the percentage of people

---

[8] Respondents are also able to answer "don't know." For these purposes, respondents who chose this answer have been dropped from the analysis.

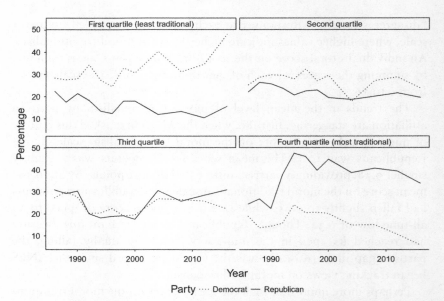

FIGURE 1.4. Partisan scores on moral traditionalism by quartile. This figure shows the trend in the percentage of Democrats and Republicans who scored in each quartile of the moral traditionalism scale.

who fall in the second quartile. There has been a 18.2% decrease in the number of Democrats who fall in the third quartile, while the percentage of Republicans scoring in this quartile in 2016 is nearly identical to the percentage of Republicans who scored in this quartile in 1986. That the partisan changes in the second and third quartiles have been small compared to the changes in the first and the fourth indicates that the divide over cultural issues has been largely driven by Democrats and Republicans gradually moving to their own party's most extreme positions.

Much like they have done with racial and cultural identities, partisans have sorted to a considerable extent along ideological lines (Abramowitz and Saunders 1998). While the Democratic and Republican parties both used to be a mix of ideological liberals and conservatives, the modern-day party system is one in which ideological liberals have found a home in the Democratic Party and ideological conservatives have claimed the Republican Party. Liberal Republicans and conservative Democrats are ever-dwindling in strength.

In 1972, 36.1% of Democrats indicated that they were ideologically liberal, 39.3% reported that they were moderate, and 24.6% reported that they were conservative. By 2016, almost 63% of Democrats identified as liberals; 27% were ideologically moderate; and, finally, just over 10% identified as conservative. Thus, over the forty-four-year period that the ANES tracked both party and ideological identification, there was a 74% increase in the number of Democrats who identified as ideologically liberal. The majority of this shift was caused by a precipitous decline in the percentage of Democrats who identify as ideologically conservative.

The trends among Republicans are a mirror image. In 1972, 53.4% of Republicans identified as ideologically conservative; 33.4% were moderate in their ideological leanings; and, finally, the remaining 13.1% identified as ideologically liberal. By 2016, an overwhelming majority of Republicans – 76.3% – identified as ideologically conservative. This increase in the number of conservative Republicans came partially at the expense of those who were ideologically moderate (down to approximately 21%) but was driven primarily by the sharp decline in the percentage of Republicans identifying as ideologically liberal. Indeed, by 2016, the percentage of liberal Republicans was a paltry 2.7%. These trends, along with the trends in ideological identification for Democrats, are shown in Figure 1.5.

The sorting of liberals into the Democratic Party and conservatives into the Republican Party has done much to produce a political environment in which supporters of one party increasingly see supporters of the opposing party as distinct from themselves. These growing differences often stem from the fact that liberals and conservatives tend to have different worldviews. One place where such differences are seen is in responses to questions that seek to measure an individual's personality. Known as the "Big Five," personality is often measured in a scholarly setting by analyzing five personality traits: openness to new experiences, agreeableness, conscientiousness, extraversion, and emotional stability (Mondak 2010). Based off of scores on the Big Five personality framework, two key elements tend to stick out: liberals often score higher than conservatives in terms of openness to new experiences; conservatives, on the other hand, tend to score higher than liberals on measures of conscientiousness. In practical terms, this means that liberals are more open to experimentation and new ideas, while conservatives prioritize self-discipline, dependability, and organization. These trends, based off of data from the 2016 ANES, are documented in Figure 1.6.

Ranging from possible values of 0–6, the trends shown in Figure 1.6 show that the most liberal individuals have a mean Conscientiousness score of 4.4. By contrast, the most conservative individuals have a mean

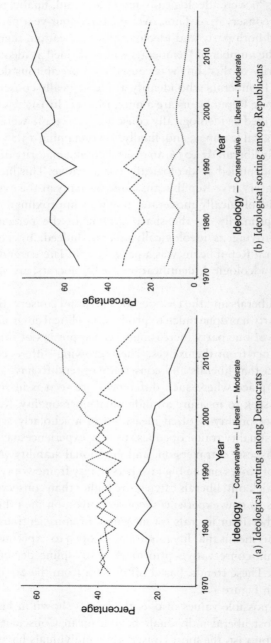

FIGURE 1.5. Partisan-ideological sorting, 1972–2016. These two subfigures show the trends in partisan-ideological sorting for the Democratic and Republican parties from 1972 to 2016.

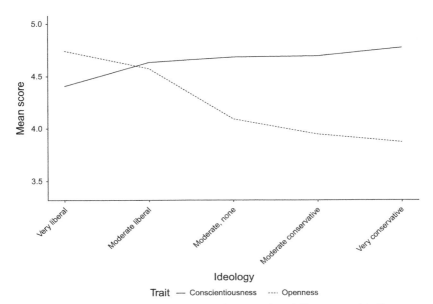

FIGURE 1.6. Ideological identification and personality differences. This figure shows the mean score on the Big Five measures of openness to new experiences and conscientiousness by an individual's ideological self-identification. Liberals tend to score higher on the openness measure while conservatives score higher on the conscientiousness measure.

Conscientiousness score of 4.8. The opposite relationship emerges when examining scores on the openness to new experiences measure. Here, it is the most liberal individuals that have the highest mean score (4.75) and the most conservative individuals that have the lowest mean score (3.87). Though these differences are small in terms of absolute differences, the fact that these measures range from just 0 to 6 suggests that the differences between conservatives and liberals on these personality traits is actually quite sizable. In fact, the differences between liberals and conservatives on these measures is so important that some have argued that political differences are driven not by "where we stand ...[on issues, but by] who we are as individuals" (Johnston, Federico, and Lavine 2017).

In addition to these personality-based differences, liberals and conservatives often diverge on responses to survey items seeking to measure individual-level dispositions toward authoritarianism. Designed to capture an individual's preference between social conformity and personal autonomy, higher scores on measures of authoritarianism have been linked to support for restricting civil liberties, support for passing laws that negatively affect religious minorities, views toward politically salient groups (such as homosexuals or evangelical Christians), and a whole host of other political attitudes (Adorno et al. 1950; Dunwoody and McFarland 2017; Feldman 2003; Hetherington and Suhay 2011; Hetherington and Weiler 2009). To measure individuals' scores on authoritarianism, scholars rely on a series of four questions that capture preferences on child rearing. Specifically, people are asked to pick one trait that they think it is more important for a child to have from each of the following pairs: (1) independence or respect for elders, (2) obedience or self-reliance, (3) being considerate or being well-behaved, and (4) having curiosity or having good manners. Selecting "respect for elders," "obedience," "being well-behaved," and "having good manners" results in the most authoritarian score possible. Possible scores range from 0 to 4. Utilizing these same questions, the ideological breakdown of authoritarianism scores is shown in Figure 1.7. Data come from the 2016 ANES.

Figure 1.7 shows that the most liberal individuals have an average authoritarianism score of 1.08. This score increases to 1.31 for those who are moderate-to-liberal. Among those who indicate a moderate ideology, the average authoritarianism score is 2.3. The average score drops to 2.27 for those with a moderate-to-conservative ideology before rising to 2.47 for those who self-identify as very conservative ideologically. Thus, the general trend suggests that the most liberal individuals are the least authoritarian and the most conservative individuals are the most authoritarian.

As the ideological sorting of the Democratic and Republican parties continues, the partisan differences in worldviews – as measured by personality traits and tendencies toward authoritarianism – are almost certain to increase. These differences, combined with the racial and cultural sorting described above, suggests that in the future it will only become easier for supporters of one party to see supporters of the other as fundamentally different from themselves along a myriad of dimensions: racial, cultural, ideological, and even phenotypical. These deep and meaningful differences produce few opportunities for mutual understanding between partisans and increase the likelihood of cross-partisan anger and mistrust (see, e.g., Allport 1954). These partisan differences, and the anger they produce, are reified by the development of a new media environment and the emergence of the Internet and new technologies. I discuss these trends below.

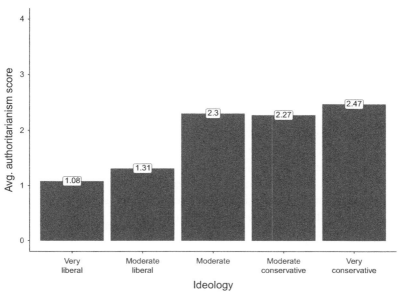

FIGURE 1.7. Ideological identification and authoritarianism. This figure shows the mean score on the authoritarianism scale by ideological self-identification.

1.4.2 A New Media Environment

The drastic change in the media landscape over the past twenty years has done much to reinforce the alignment of racial, cultural, and ideological identities with partisanship. As Prior (2007) notes, the advent of the contemporary "post-broadcast democracy" has both created a gap in terms of what citizens know about politics and ossified deeply held partisan identities. Quite simply, the incredible expansion in the media landscape has done a considerable amount to polarize the American political system and perpetuate a new style of political anger.

Data from a 2014 report by the Pew Research Center bears this out. According to the Pew study, there is a stark ideological divide in terms of what media sources individuals perceive to be trustworthy. For instance, among those who are "consistently conservative" in their ideological viewpoint, 88% said they trust Fox News to accurately and fairly report the news. By contrast, 81% of those who are "consistently liberal" in their ideology say they do *not* trust Fox News. Such differential patterns of trust in media organizations has led to a partisan and ideological divide in terms of where news is consumed: Republicans overwhelmingly favor

Fox News, while Democrats favor a mix of National Public Radio, PBS, and various TV outlets.[9]

Yet, if it is true that the rapid expansion of the media landscape has helped to perpetuate partisan polarization in the United States, the question one must ask is simple: how? The primary way that the media landscape serves to polarize the American public is by catering to the extreme partisan and ideological preferences of its audience. As previous works have shown, the polarized media landscape creates a set of "echo chambers" that allows partisans to self-select the news that best fits their predispositions (Arceneaux and Johnson 2013; Iyengar and Hahn 2009; Levendusky 2013). This process of reinforcing already-held beliefs, along with the slight amount of persuasive power it possesses (Martin and Yurukoglu 2017), makes the media a powerful institution in contemporary American politics.

One of the most straightforward ways the media serves to reinforce individuals' predispositions is by carefully selecting the guests and commentators it presents on its shows. An analysis of the relationship between the ideological extremity of Members of Congress and news mentions in *The New York Times* and on CBS evening news shows indicates that, among members of the House of Representatives, ideological extremity is positively associated with the number of media appearances (Wagner and Gruszczynski 2017). Put more succinctly, the media has a preference for ideologically extreme Members of Congress.[10] In an era in which Americans are prone to the reception of cues from political elites (Layman and Carsey 2002), the fact that ideologically extreme Members of Congress receive a disproportionate amount of media coverage vis-à-vis more moderate politicians means that, increasingly, citizens are receiving ideologically extreme viewpoints packaged in anger-inducing soundbites.

While the creation of echo chambers and the catering to tastes via the strategic booking of ideologically extreme Members of Congress helps to perpetuate anger within the electorate via the reinforcement of partisan, racial, cultural, and ideological identities, the media can serve as an

---

[9] The full report can be found at http://assets.pewresearch.org/wp-content/uploads/sites/13/2014/10/Political-Polarization-and-Media-Habits-FINAL-REPORT-7-27-15.pdf. Accessed April 17, 2018.

[10] The authors note that, though both extreme right-leaning and extreme left-leaning Members of Congress are prioritized in media appearances, the media appears to prefer ideological extremity on the political right.

anger-inducing agent on its own. Numerous studies have shown that television segments can produce anger (Holbert and Hansen 2008; Newhagen 1998) and "physiologically arouse" viewers through the presentation of incivility and "in-your-face" debate segments (Mutz 2015). As such, the style and tone of the contemporary media landscape is inherently anger-inducing. This point will be revisited in greater detail in Chapter 2.

1.4.3 Technology and the Internet

In a fashion similar to the media, the growth of the Internet and new technologies has also served to increase anger within the American electorate. Much like the modern-day TV landscape, the Internet has reinforced partisan identities through the creation of a panoply of partisan and ideologically friendly websites and social networks. As such, Americans can completely shield themselves from websites and news outlets that express discordant views, while simultaneously self-selecting into online news sources that espouse ideologically extreme viewpoints.

The trend toward the consumption of news via the Internet has increased considerably in the past few years. According to a 2016 poll conducted by Gallup, 15% of Americans aged 18–34 reported that their primary source of news was an Internet website. Though this number may appear small, its growth has been exponential: indeed, just three years earlier Gallup found that only 3% of individuals in this same age cohort listed an Internet website as their first stop for news about politics and current affairs.[11] This turn toward the consumption of news from online sources has potentially troubling consequences for political behavior, as a growing body of research suggests that individuals seek self-consistency by means of the websites they view. In other words, the act of reading news on the Internet is done to reinforce and solidify one's already-held political views (Dvir-Gvirsman 2016; Pariser 2011).

This desire for homophily – the preference to be surrounded by like-minded individuals – extends beyond patterns of behavior involving Internet news websites. In fact, the trend is exacerbated when one examines social media and related websites (Sunstein 2001). One groundbreaking study found that Facebook users were exposed to very little cross-cutting

---

[11] The full study, titled "Americans Increasingly Turn to Specific Sources for News," can be found in full at http://news.gallup.com/poll/193553/americans-increasingly-turn-specific-sources-news.aspx.

ideological content. Instead, most Facebook users saw news shared by their friends that fit with their own political views. Because "partisans tend to maintain relationships with like-minded contacts" and the content one is exposed to on Facebook depends largely on these contacts, users are most frequently exposed to ideologically confirming information (Bakshy, Messing, and Adamic 2015).

Even more troubling than individuals' self-selecting online behavior is the tendency for individuals to be exposed to and consume fake news online. One recent study suggested that nearly 25% of Americans visited a fake news website during the 2016 presidential election, though the most frequent visits were confined to a smaller subgroup of the population. Though not exclusively, most of these visits to fake news websites came from links via Facebook. Worryingly, attempts to alleviate the consequences of fake news consumption appears to be unsuccessful. Indeed, the presence of fact checks on fallacious news stories was unable to prevent the acceptance of false narratives (Guess, Nyhan, and Reifler 2018).

Homophilous behavior on the Internet extends further than just news websites and social media. In fact, the current political climate has given rise to a considerable number of niche online dating services that specialize in matching individuals with similar political beliefs. Republican singles interested in dating someone with like-minded political beliefs can choose from sites such as conservativesonly.com, trumpsingles.com, or republicanpeoplemeet.com. Similarly, Democrats looking for a relationship can peruse liberalhearts.com, democraticpeoplemeet.com, or democratsingles.com. With 28% of people saying they would no longer date someone from the opposing political party, such websites cater to a growing political niche in terms of online dating.[12] This also comports with recent evidence that suggests that parents would be disappointed if their child married someone from the opposing party (Iyengar, Sood, and Lelkes 2012).

1.5 POLITICAL ELITES AND AMERICAN RAGE

The primary argument of this book is that the trends in public opinion and political behavior described in Section 1.3 – declining trust in government, a weakening commitment to democratic norms, and higher

---

[12] See the "Singles in America" report from Match.com for more details: www.multivu .com/players/English/8264851-match-singles-in-america-study/.

degrees of partisan loyalty in voting behavior – have been perpetuated and exacerbated by rising levels of anger within the electorate. This anger has developed over time through the process of partisan sorting along racial, cultural, and ideological dimensions. This process has made it easy for supporters of one party to see supporters of the opposing party as "the other" along multiple dimensions. These stark and deep differences reduce the potential for cross-partisan understanding and increase the probability that Democrats and Republicans view each other through the lens of anger. Moreover, this anger is reinforced by a media environment and a host of websites and associated technologies that allow partisans to self-select into environments that offer friendly viewpoints.

The emergence of this culture of rage among the electorate offers political elites the opportunity to strategically stoke and elicit anger for their own purposes. Examining whether elites engage in such behavior, and whether there is a periodicity to their elicitation of anger, is the task to which I now turn.

2

Political Elites and the Strategic Use of Anger

> Anyone can become angry – that is easy …
> — Aristotle

In Chapter 1, I argued that partisan sorting along racial, cultural, and ideological lines, combined with the emergence of a new media landscape and the development of the Internet, has led to a political environment in which it is easy for supporters of one party to see supporters of the other as increasingly different from themselves. These clear and deep differences often proscribe opportunities for partisans to learn about those who think differently from themselves and, more often than not, lead to situations where anger is omnipresent. If political elites are cognizant of this anger and its ability to affect public opinion and voter behavior, eliciting anger could be used by political elites for strategic purposes. Accordingly, in this chapter I examine whether elites do, in fact, stoke anger for strategic purposes. Moreover, I examine whether there is a periodicity to this trend.

The results of the analyses in this chapter suggest that political elites strategically engage in behavior that is designed to elicit anger within the electorate toward the opposing political party, its supporters, and its governing elite. I first show this through an analysis of every message sent by presidential candidates on Twitter (known as a "tweet") during the 2016 presidential campaign. Next, I analyze the transcripts of nearly every TV show that aired on Fox News and MSNBC between 1999 and 2016 to show that partisan media outlets deliberately stoke anger among their viewers. I also find that political elites increase their anger-inducing rhetoric around key points of the political calendar and in response to the emergence of noteworthy politicians. In total, the evidence I present here suggests that political elites – whether conceptualized as politicians or media figures – are not innocent bystanders to the prominent role of anger in American political behavior. On the contrary, political elites are deliberately encouraging their supporters to be angry.

2.1 ELITES AND THE INVOCATION OF ANGER

2.1.1 Historical Trends

American political history is full of candidates whose stump speeches and campaign events were designed to elicit anger among their audience. As early as the election of 1800, political candidates and their partisan-affiliated institutions were engaging in incessant demagoguery. Newspapers supporting John Adams and the Federalists warned that Thomas Jefferson's Democratic Republicans had "the devil in their hearts," were American Jacobins, and a vote cast for the party's slate of candidates would be akin to "rebelling against Heaven." A decade later, a prominent newspaper affiliated with the Democratic Republicans accused the Federalists of being treasonous for not sufficiently supporting the War of 1812. Similarly, the Democratic Republican-aligned *National Intelligencer* informed its readers that the Massachusetts state legislature was full of nothing but "seditious blusterings."[1]

Arguably the most famous example of anger in politics from this period of time – and perhaps in all of early American politics – is the heated rivalry between Aaron Burr and Alexander Hamilton. Two leaders of the nascent republic, the men were separated by a massive political and philosophical divide. Vice President to Thomas Jefferson and an important political figure in his own right, Burr helped to lead a party dedicated to agrarianism and states' rights. Hamilton, meanwhile, was the early republic's signal articulator of mercantilism and a strong federal government. These differences, compounded by bitter political battles and fits of anger, eventually led Burr to fatally shoot Hamilton on July 11, 1804. Hamilton's death one day later would accurately, if not ironically, confirm his earlier observation that "men are …for the most part governed by the impulse of passion."[2]

---

[1] Quotes excerpted from Larson (2007).
[2] Quoted from Chernow (2005).

Such "impulse of passion" would not go away with Hamilton's death. The election of 1824, contested by John Quincy Adams and Andrew Jackson, was so divided that its ultimate resolution had to be determined by a vote in the House of Representatives. There, Henry Clay convinced his faction of supporters in the House to vote for Adams's candidacy. Such support was enough to swing the presidency in Adams's favor. In return, Adams named Clay as his Secretary of State. Jackson's supporters, irate that the candidate who won the popular vote nevertheless did not win the presidency, dubbed the arrangement between Adams and Clay a "corrupt bargain." What was known as the "era of good feelings," so deemed for its lack of two-party competition in the wake of the Federalists' demise, was in actuality anything but tranquil. On the contrary, the interparty anger between the Democratic Republicans and the Federalists that had characterized the early years of the country's political history had shifted to intraparty anger within the Democratic Republican ranks as the party of Jefferson increasingly became the party of Jackson.

Approximately thirty years later, partisan anger reached even higher levels. In fact, anger within Congress was at such extraordinarily high levels that physical violence ensued. During an impassioned speech on the floor of the Senate, Charles Sumner, a Republican from Massachusetts, denounced slavery as an inhumane institution that was unbecoming of the country. Sumner's denunciations were acutely directed toward Andrew Butler, a Democratic senator from South Carolina and an ardent supporter of slavery. Upset by Sumner's remarks toward Butler and about the institution of slavery, Preston Brooks, a congressman from South Carolina and relative of Butler, stormed into the Senate chamber and began to attack Sumner with his cane. According to the report issued by the Senate Select Committee investigating the attack, Brooks found Sumner sitting at his desk and began to "assault him with considerable violence, striking him numerous blows on and about the head with a walking stick, which cut his head and disabled him for the time being from attending to his duties in the Senate."[3]

The "Caning of Charles Sumner," as the event would come to be known, turned out to be a precursor to the Civil War. The most deadly conflict in American history, the Civil War was sparked by Southern anger

---

[3] The entire report of the Senate Select Committee's investigation into this incident, issued May 28, 1856, can be read in full at www.senate.gov/artandhistory/history/resources/pdf/ SumnerInvestigation1856.pdf.

over the increasing unease in the North toward slavery. This unease, compounded by the election of Abraham Lincoln to the presidency, pushed the Southern states to the conclusion that the only possible way to defend their society's fundamental institution was through outright hostilities. Anger in the wake of the Civil War's conclusion would lead to Jim Crow laws in the South that ensured that, though slavery was abolished de jure, the social hierarchy in the Southern United States reflected a de facto system of Black subjugation.

Countless other examples of anger dot the landscape of American political history. Indeed, as the nineteenth century gave way to the twentieth, the permanence and importance of anger in American politics continued to be illustrated by events such as the Teapot Dome scandal during the Harding administration, and the Great Depression and the march of the "Bonus Army." Perhaps most contentious were the events of the 1960s, which saw wide-scale protests against the nation's military involvement in Vietnam and other Southeast Asian countries. Spurred on by protests from college faculty and students, anger-fueled demonstrations against the war soon spread beyond campus. Indeed, in April 1966, approximately 5,000 protesters gathered in New York City's Times Square and another 4,000 congregated in Berkeley, California, to express their frustration with the conflict (Wells 1994). This public anger with the war both shaped and was reinforced by elite anger, with liberals such as George McGovern accusing the Nixon White House of being "evil" in their prosecution of the war. In a contentious step that aroused anger on both sides of the political divide, McGovern took the further step of comparing the barbarism of the American war effort to Nazi Germany's actions during the Holocaust (Webb 1995). Thus, Vietnam had become, in the words of Senator Ed Muskie, "a bleeding sore" that elicited anger at both the elite and mass levels of American politics (DeBenedetti 1990).

Such discontent was accompanied by the fusion between anger, race, and education in the 1960s and 1970s – fueled by the Supreme Court's ruling in *Swann* v. *Charlotte-Mecklenburg Board of Education* – that saw the government attempt to desegregate public schools by busing students across school districts. In her contemporary account of busing in the Richmond (California) Unified School District, Rubin (1972) argued that "busing school children to correct racial imbalance is perhaps the hottest issue in American politics, and public retribution against those who favor busing plans is swift and sure." Such retribution and anger did come, with Richard Nixon calling busing "divisive" and "a bad means to a good end."[4] Such language was not an isolated incident; on the contrary, it was a key part of Nixon's "Southern Strategy" of galvanizing White anger and racial resentment against African Americans. Such resentment has not abated with the passage of time. Indeed, discussions about racial equality and the federal government's practice of busing African American students to White school districts were points of contention in the 2020 Democratic presidential primary debates (Hannah-Jones 2019).

2.1.2 Anger in the Contemporary Era

Though American political history is replete with anger, as the preceding discussion has shown, the past two decades of American politics have been particularly acrimonious. Prompted by the 2001 and 2003 Republican tax cuts, as well as the wars in Afghanistan and Iraq, Democrats campaigning for Congress in 2006 launched attacks on Republican candidates all across the country. Employing a strategy that labeled Republicans as "corrupt" and "incompetent," Democrats rode a wave of anger in the electorate to their first congressional majority in over a decade.[5] Yet, the anger that propelled Democrats into the majority in both the House of Representatives and the Senate would not abate with the 2006 election. On the contrary, the Democrats' stunning electoral victories, combined with Republican frustrations with the perceived lavishness of the George W. Bush administration, led to the beginnings of the Tea Party movement within the Republican Party.

The Tea Party movement reached its apex in 2010. Buoyed by extreme anger toward Barack Obama, a floundering economy, the fight for health care expansion, and Republicans deemed to be insufficiently conservative (nicknamed RINOs, or "Republicans in Name Only"), the Tea Party organized contentious marches and protests all across the country. However, arguing that the Tea Party was purely an economically rational reaction to a poor economy and perceived government overreach would be incorrect. As Williamson, Skocpol, and Coggin (2011) note, while the Tea Party was driven by anger toward the proposed expansion of government services and programs, such anger was able to coexist with "considerable acceptance, even warmth, toward long-standing federal social programs

---

[4] Nixon's speech on school busing can be read in full at: www.nytimes.com/1972/03/17/archives/transcript-of-nixons-statement-on-school-busing.html.

[5] See this report from *The Washington Post* for details on Democrats' messaging strategy during the 2006 campaign: www.washingtonpost.com/wp-dyn/content/article/2006/11/09/AR2006110900147.html.

like Social Security and Medicare." The reconciliation to this apparent contradiction in support for government programs and services is that the Tea Party's anger was directed at the provision of such goods and services to those who were seen as "the other." Given the Tea Party's sociodemographic makeup, "the other" for Tea Party supporters was the growing percentage of the American population that is non-White and not Protestant (Skocpol and Williamson 2016). Accordingly, the roots of the Tea Party movement were to be found in the anger and frustration of a segment of the American population that was nostalgic for the (real or imagined) decades of the past.

Recent work by Jones (2016) cogently illustrates how this desire for the past influences contemporary political behavior. Jones argues that demographic and societal changes in the country have led to the declining political power of White Christian conservatives, a trend he calls the "death of White Christian America." While once a powerful voting bloc and a "notable ...cultural touchstone" for American society, the tenets of White Christian Americans increasingly clashed with a society becoming more racially diverse and more liberal on social issues. This diminished political power, combined with – and precipitated by – a growing non-White population in the United States, has led to a politics of backlash among White Christian Americans.

This backlash reached its pinnacle during the 2016 election. Indeed, Donald Trump, the Republican nominee, was explicit in his appeal to those Americans who felt left behind by social and demographic changes. His campaign slogan, "Make America Great Again," was designed specifically to make people think back on previous eras of American history and yearn for this past. Tapping into the myth of American exceptionalism and Ronald Reagan's idealization of the United States as a "shining city on a hill," Trump cogently argued that only by returning to the values and societal structure of previous decades could the country be made great again.

Though the Trump campaign slogan was vague in nature, subsequent polls indicate that Trump's supporters had strong opinions as to when America was at its greatest. Though most Trump supporters pointed to the year 2000 as a time when the country was great, the second most referenced year was 1955.[6] This number is significant for the idea that

---

[6] These findings are the result of a Morning Consult poll conducted seven months prior to the 2016 general election. For an analysis of the poll, see this report in *The New York Times*: www.nytimes.com/2016/04/26/upshot/when-was-america-greatest.html. Accessed May 2, 2018.

Trump's electoral success was built on a wave of angry backlash against social and demographic trends reshaping the country. Data from the 1950 Census – the best estimates as to the racial breakdown of the country in 1955 – indicate that 89.5% of people living in the United States were White and 10% were Black. By 2015, government data indicates that these percentages had changed to 79% and 13%, respectively. Over this same time period, the non-White percentage of the population doubled (moving from 10.5% in the 1950s to 21% in 2015).[7]

At the same time, fewer Americans are identifying as Christians and an increasing amount are identifying as atheist or agnostic. Polling data from Gallup indicates that more than 90% of Americans self-identified with some denomination of Christianity in the 1950s. By 2015, the percentage of Americans who self-identified as Christians had dropped to 75% and the percentage of "religious nones" had risen to just under 20%.[8] Though these numbers indicate that the country is still overwhelmingly Christian, this represents a nearly 17% decline in the number of people claiming adherence to the faith.

These demographic and societal shifts are important because Trump's base of support in the 2016 election was overwhelmingly White and Christian. National exit polls indicate that Trump won 58% of the vote from White Americans. Additionally, 81% of those who identified as an "evangelical" or "born-again" Christian voted for Trump.[9] In fact, Trump's level of support among evangelical Christians topped that of any other previous Republican presidential candidate (Smith and Martinez 2016). This support has remained steady into his first term, especially among White evangelicals; among this subgroup, nearly 75% approved of Trump's job performance in an April 2018 Public Religion Research Institute poll compared to 42% of the general population.[10] That White Americans and evangelical Christians supported, and continue to

---

[7] The historical collection of the Statistical Abstract of the United States, which contains data from the US Census Bureau and other government organizations, can be downloaded at www.census.gov/library/publications/time-series/statistical_abstracts.html. Accessed August 8, 2018.

[8] This data can be found at http://news.gallup.com/poll/187955/percentage-christians-drifting-down-high.aspx. Accessed May 2, 2018.

[9] National exit poll results can be found via *The New York Times*: www.nytimes.com/interactive/2016/11/08/us/politics/election-exit-polls.html?mtrref=www.google.com. Accessed May 2, 2018.

[10] This study can be found at www.prri.org/spotlight/white-evangelical-support-for-donald-trump-at-all-time-high/. Accessed May 3, 2018.

support, Trump in such numbers suggests that their political decision making was motivated by anger about the aforementioned changes in terms of demographics and religiosity within the country.

Recent work indicates that this anger about societal and demographic changes did, in fact, play a key role in predicting mass-level support for Trump. Utilizing novel data from Michigan, a state that was essential to Trump's victory in the Electoral College, Grossmann and Thaler (2018) utilize respondents' level of agreement or disagreement to a two-item questionnaire to build a scale that measures "aversion to change." The questions used were: (1) "Our country is changing too fast, undermining traditional American values" and (2) "By accepting diverse cultures and lifestyles, our country is steadily improving." The results of their analysis suggest that those individuals who exhibited more aversion to change were more likely to support Trump than Clinton during the 2016 election. While causality cannot be determined from Grossmann and Thaler's (2018) data, the results are nevertheless indicative of the link between anger and concern over societal and demographic changes and support for Trump (see also, Craig and Richeson 2017).

While White Americans and evangelical Christians offered Trump high levels of support in the 2016 election due to their belief that the country was changing in ways that were detrimental to their societal standing, Hillary Clinton's supporters were more inclined to believe that the country had not changed drastically enough. For instance, 72% of Clinton supporters agreed with the claim that women still face "significant obstacles" that make it harder for them to get ahead compared to men, and 55% agreed that racial discrimination still prevents Black people from social and professional achievement (Smith 2016). That Trump supporters think the country has moved too far away from its social moorings while Clinton supporters think the country has not gone far enough explains why both Democrats and Republicans think their party has been "losing" more political debates than it "wins." According to a recent report by the Pew Research Center, 53% of Republicans and 78% of Democrats believe that their side loses more than wins in terms of political issues discussed over the past few years.[11]

The high stakes and perceived victimhood on both sides of the political divide led to highly charged elite discourse during the 2016 general

---

[11] The report, "Key findings on Americans' views of the U.S. political system and democracy," can be found at www.pewresearch.org/fact-tank/2018/04/26/key-findings-on-americans-views-of-the-u-s-political-system-and-democracy/. Accessed May 3, 2018.

election that sought to induce anger among the electorate. Trump and Clinton were constantly exchanging insults and verbal jabs throughout the course of the campaign. With Trump frequently referring to Clinton as "Crooked Hillary" and Clinton responding by calling Trump's supporters a "basket of deplorables," the 2016 election was noteworthy for its negativity. So great was the level of anger and hostility that the London-based *The Daily Telegraph* offered this assessment:[12]

He calls her "unhinged" and "rotten." She calls him "dangerous" and a "bully." All elections have their bitter moments, but this year's bid to the most powerful office in the world has sunk to unprecedented lows. As the American presidential election careers towards voting day, with less than two months to go, sober policy discussion has been drowned out by personal insults and base offensives.

Even after his election to the presidency, Donald Trump continued his attempts to keep his base angry. One tactic Trump employed was his perpetual claim that media reports unflattering to him were "biased," "fake," a "hoax," or part of a "witch hunt" against his administration (Glasser 2019). These claims were often – and most vociferously – directed toward Robert Mueller, who was appointed as Special Counsel in 2017 to investigate the Russian government's attempts to influence the 2016 presidential election, and his team of lawyers (Abrams 2019). Such anger-inducing rhetoric was also applied to what Trump and his supporters labeled the "deep state," a group of government bureaucrats who were supposedly committed to overthrowing Trump's presidency (Taub and Fisher 2017). And, despite his electoral victory over her in the 2016 election, Trump continued to elicit anger among his supporters toward Hillary Clinton with incessant calls at his rallies to "lock her up" for being "crooked" (Frazin 2019). Such anger appears to have had an effect, with Republicans expressing overwhelming distrust in the media and a disliking for Trump's political opponents (Gilberstadt 2019; Gottfried, Stocking, and Grieco 2018).

2.2 ANGER AS AN ESSENTIAL FUNCTION OF CANDIDATE PERFORMANCE

Clearly, American politicians have long sought to invoke anger. But why have politicians throughout history sought to arouse anger among the

---

[12] The full story can be found at www.telegraph.co.uk/news/2016/09/17/us-election-2016-welcome-to-americas-unpopularity-contest/. Accessed April 26, 2018.

public? To understand such a question, it is helpful to first understand what politicians are thought to do. According to Mayhew's (1974) classic formulation, congressmen's overarching concern is to be reelected. To achieve this end they undertake three key activities: advertising, credit claiming, and position taking. Fundamentally, advertising refers to the ways in which politicians increase their name recognition. This can occur via canvassing, direct mailing, or, in the modern era, email campaigns. Credit claiming deals with congressional officials attempting to signal their effectiveness in office. Such appeals are meant to strengthen the individual bonds between a congressman and his constituents by showing what he has personally done for his district. Finally, position taking is a strategy politicians undertake in an attempt to situate themselves in some ideological space. Such placement should minimize the difference between the politician's policy preferences and those of the constituency he represents.

Recent studies argue that, in addition to advertising, credit claiming, and position taking, politicians engage in a fourth strategy: "partisan taunting" (Grimmer 2013; Grimmer and King 2011). Partisan taunting is so prevalent that "when engaging the same topics, the parties articulate distinctive positions and often espouse vitriol at the other party." Studying the debates in the US Senate over the American military's invasion of Iraq in 2004, Grimmer (2013) argues that it is the most conservative Republicans and the most liberal Democrats who are most likely to engage in this vitriolic speech (for additional evidence on ideological extremity and negative speech, see Frimer et al. n.d.). These polarized senators are able to do this, he argues, because they are ideologically in line with their constituencies and, therefore, are electorally safe. Conversely, those senators who are in electorally competitive districts tend to focus their communications on credit claiming and highlighting the ways in which they have been successful on behalf of their constituents. These distinct patterns of political messaging have led to what Grimmer (2013) calls an "artificially polarized discourse."

Regardless of the conditions necessary for "partisan taunting" to be successfully employed, the fact that such a campaign tactic exists for some subset of politicians suggests that candidates for elected office are aware that anger can be strategically used to mobilize and motivate the electorate. In an era defined by negative partisanship and affective polarization (Abramowitz and Webster 2016; Iyengar and Westwood 2015; Rogowski and Sutherland 2015), the incentive to engage in such "partisan taunting" is likely to be at its apogee. Thus, an analysis of elite speech should reveal patterns that indicate a concerted effort to arouse anger within the electorate in order to further a candidate's own electoral ends.

2.3 ANGER AND CANDIDATE RHETORIC IN 2016

To examine how candidates use rhetoric designed to elicit anger among the electorate, I analyzed every message sent via Twitter (known as a "tweet") by candidates during the 2016 general election. One of the more popular social media websites, Twitter played an outsized role in the 2016 election due to Donald Trump's prolific use of the platform. Though there are many possible data sources to rely upon in order to analyze the ways in which candidates employ anger-inducing rhetoric, using Twitter is beneficial for a number of reasons. First, almost every candidate who ran for President during the 2016 cycle had a Twitter account.[13] Thus, using Twitter affords me the ability to compare and contrast the ways in which each candidate sought to use anger-inducing rhetoric. Second, using Twitter data is beneficial because of its character limits. Because each tweet can be a maximum of only 140 characters, each message that a candidate sends must be direct and to the point.[14] Rather than expounding on a point as one might do in a campaign speech, tweets force candidates to distill their message to the central idea. Finally, because each tweet is timestamped, I am able to track how the use of anger-inducing rhetoric via Twitter ebbs and flows over the course of the campaign.

One concern with using Twitter data in order to determine the extent to which politicians seek to elicit anger among their supporters is that many of these politicians' supporters likely did not – and still do not – use Twitter. In this case, it is possible that politicians may be sending anger-inducing messages but very few people are actually receiving these cues. Indeed, the majority of the American public is not active on Twitter. However, research from the field of Communications suggests that those Americans who do not use Twitter are still likely to be exposed

---

[13] Though using Twitter data provides wide coverage in terms of candidates, it is unlikely that the candidates themselves were responsible for each tweet that was sent from their account. Indeed, it is more probable that each candidate's campaign staff tasked an individual or group of individuals with maintaining the candidate's social media presence. However, as has been shown with speechwriters and Members of Congress, it is likely that these staffers wrote tweets that were in line with both the candidate's message and lexical style.

[14] Twitter expanded the limit to 280 characters per tweet in November 2017.

to the content of politicians' tweets. This is because political journalists are heavy users of Twitter (Lawrence et al. 2014; Mourão 2014) and tend to view tweets as newsworthy (McGregor and Molyneux 2018). Accordingly, political journalists are likely to reference politicians' tweets in their news stories and, in some cases, include direct links to the tweets themselves. The result is that these anger-inducing cues are spread beyond Twitter and are received by those who are not users of the platform.

The data for this analysis includes both the Republican and Democratic primary elections, as well as the general election between Donald Trump and Hillary Clinton. Pooled together, this represents 114,222 tweets. Over 83,393 of these tweets were sent by Republicans while the remaining 30,829 were sent by Democrats. A full list of the candidates in this dataset, as well as the number of tweets each candidate sent, is shown in Table 2.1.

To begin, I analyzed the degree to which each candidate sent anger-inducing tweets throughout the presidential primary season and how this varied over time. As a simplifying assumption, a candidate's tweet is classified as "anger-inducing" if it specifically mentions one of his or her opponents. Of course, measuring anger-inducing tweets in this way is a particular choice. Like all methodological or classification choices, this

TABLE 2.1 *Twitter activity in the 2016 election*

Candidate	No. of Tweets
Ben Carson	6,261
Bernie Sanders	14,475
Carly Fiorina	6,508
Chris Christie	12,155
Donald Trump	7,829
Hillary Clinton	9,727
Jeb Bush	6,549
Jim Gilmore	3,401
John Kasich	6,757
Marco Rubio	6,711
Martin O'Malley	6,627
Mike Huckabee	6,637
Rand Paul	6,860
Rick Santorum	6,529
Ted Cruz	7,196

This table displays summary statistics for Twitter usage by presidential candidates in 2016.

approach entails trade-offs. However, relying on tweets where the candidates mention their opponent by name as a classification rule for anger-inducing tweets is useful for two reasons. First, it is likely to accurately capture the intent behind the tweet. Indeed, it is difficult to imagine a tweet where Clinton, Trump, or some other candidate specifically named another candidate and offered a compliment or a flattering piece of analysis. On the contrary, candidates who mention their opponent are oftentimes (if not exclusively) doing so precisely because they are attempting to direct anger toward the opponent (for evidence of this, see Rhodes and Vayo 2018). Second, using this approach as a classification scheme for anger-inducing tweets is useful because, if anything, it is a conservative approach. It is possible that a candidate might send a tweet that is meant to elicit anger that does not mention the opposing candidate by name. However, by omitting such tweets from the classification scheme, the results presented in this chapter can be seen as a lower bound on the number of anger-inducing tweets that candidates sent during the course of the campaign.

Another concern is that this simplifying assumption captures candidates' attempts to arouse a multitude of negative emotions, such as anger, anxiety, and fear. While it is reasonable to assume that candidates do attempt to elicit anxiety or fear among the electorate, it is likely that anger is the emotion candidates are most frequently attempting to stir within the electorate. Anxiety, for instance, may cause individuals to seek out new information but it is also likely to dissuade individuals from participating in the political process (see, e.g., Albertson and Gadarian 2015). By contrast, anger is a more action-oriented emotion that often prompts the person experiencing the anger to engage in some action or set of actions that assuages their rage (Averill 1982). Rather than seeking to turn voters off from the political process by appealing to anxiety, political elites seek to encourage the electorate into taking an action – such as voting, canvassing, or donating money – that benefits themselves. Anger, and not anxiety or fear, is the emotion most able to accomplish this goal. Thus, the behavioral implications of negative emotions and the strategic calculus facing political actors suggests that elites are most commonly seeking to elicit anger.

Relying on the simplifying assumption described above, the aggregate number of anger-inducing tweets sent by Republican candidates during the 2016 presidential primaries is shown in Figure 2.1. The mean number of anger-inducing tweets sent during the primary season is 3.2, a relatively small number reflective of the fact that the vast majority of candidate

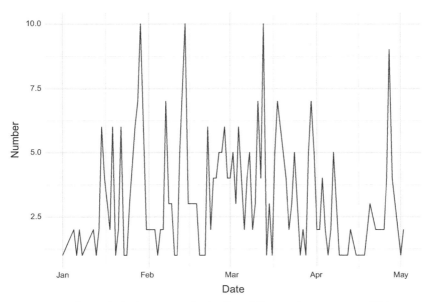

FIGURE 2.1. Anger-inducing tweets in the Republican primary season. This figure shows the number of anger-inducing tweets sent per day during the 2016 Republican primary campaign.

tweets sent during this period of the campaign largely focused on promoting one's personal brand or announcing details of campaign stops. However, the time series shown in Figure 2.1 does contain several spikes. This indicates that certain events throughout the Republican primary season prompted the candidates to increase the number of anger-inducing tweets they sent.

The first large spike occurred on January 29, 2016. This day was important in the overall landscape of the Republican primary season because it was three days before the Iowa caucus. As the first state to cast votes during the presidential election cycle, winning the Iowa caucuses is of great importance. Accordingly, candidates increased their anger-inducing tweets in an attempt to galvanize their supporters. The second large spike occurred on February 14, 2016. This was five days after the New Hampshire primary and six days before the South Carolina primary. Thus, it came on the heels of the nation's first primary and just before the first primary south of the Mason-Dixon line. The third spike came on March 13, 2016, just two days before the set of primaries held on "Super Tuesday 2." Florida, Illinois, Missouri, North Carolina, Ohio, and the Northern Mariana Islands all held primaries on this day, meaning 366 delegates

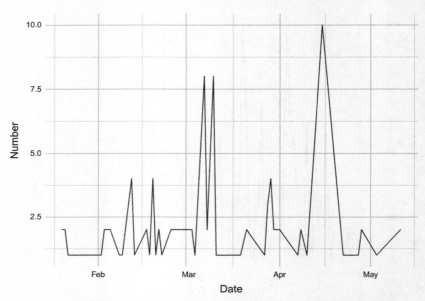

FIGURE 2.2. Anger-inducing tweets in the Democratic primary season. This figure shows the number of anger-inducing tweets sent per day during the 2016 Democratic primary campaign.

were up for grabs. The final spike came on April 27, 2016, which was the day after the so-called Acela primary involving voting in Connecticut, Delaware, Maryland, Pennsylvania, and Rhode Island. Thus, Republicans' anger-inducing tweets during the presidential primaries showed a persistent pattern of increasing around election days.

Much like the trends observed among the Republicans, anger-inducing tweets sent by Democratic candidates during the primary season tended to rise around particularly salient events. The number of anger-inducing tweets sent by candidates during the Democratic primary cycle is shown in Figure 2.2. Three spikes characterize this time series. The first spike occurred on March 7, 2016, one day after a debate between Hillary Clinton and Bernie Sanders in Flint, Michigan. The second spike came soon after on March 10, 2016 – one day after a debate hosted by Univision in Miami, Florida. The third major spike in the time series occurred on April 15, 2016. As with the first two spikes, this increase in anger-inducing tweets came one day after the last debate of the primary season. Thus, unlike their Republican counterparts, Democratic candidates tended to increase their anger-inducing tweets in the wake of televised debates.

As with the patterns observed in the tweets sent during the Republican and Democratic primary elections, the messages that Donald Trump and Hillary Clinton sent during the general election suggest that both were attempting to strategically use their Twitter accounts in order to elicit anger among their followers. However, unlike the small number of anger-inducing tweets sent during the primary season, the quantity of anger-inducing tweets sent during the general election was quite large. Trump's tweets, for instance, suggest a concerted effort to arouse anger toward Hillary Clinton and the Democratic Party. While Trump's most frequently Tweeted words were attempting to direct focus on himself ("Trump," "will," and "great") as well as his campaign's theme ("make America great again"), a distinct pattern of attacking Clinton and her candidacy is clearly present in the data. Trump mentioned "Hillary" 778 times, "Clinton" 494 times, and "crooked" (referring to "Crooked Hillary Clinton," his disparaging nickname for Clinton) 393 times.

Similarly, Hillary Clinton's campaign used her Twitter account to direct her followers' attention toward Donald Trump. In fact, Clinton's most frequently tweeted word was "Trump" (1,822 mentions). Clinton referred to "Donald" an additional 836 times. Beyond this, Clinton's tweets largely focused on issues and social groups. Examples include "families" (373 times), "women" (437 times), "plan" (321 times), and "work" (420 times).

More instructive than the raw number of tweets or the raw number of anger-inducing tweets that the candidates sent is how the volume of such tweets varied over the course of the campaign.[15] To the extent that candidates are responsive to the ever-changing nature of an electoral campaign, we should expect to see variation in the number of tweets and the number of anger-inducing tweets sent by each candidate per day. Additionally, we should expect to see the volume of tweets and anger-inducing tweets increase after salient campaign events. The trend in both the number of tweets and the number of anger-inducing tweets sent by each candidate per day are shown in Figures 2.3 and 2.4, respectively. The total number of tweets are calculated by simply summing the number of tweets sent per candidate per day, while anger-inducing tweets are calculated by summing the number of times Trump tweeted in reference to "Clinton," "Hillary," or "Crooked" (or any combination of these things), and Clinton tweeted in reference to "Donald," "Trump," or a combination of the two.

---

[15] For these purposes, I designate the general election campaign as starting on August 1, 2018. This date is four days after the conclusion of the Democratic National Convention, which commenced five weeks after the start of the Republican National Convention.

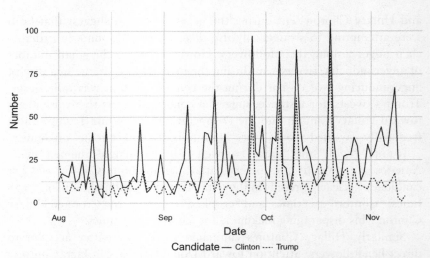

FIGURE 2.3. Donald Trump's and Hillary Clinton's tweet volume by day. This figure shows the number of tweets sent by Donald Trump and Hillary Clinton by day over the course of the general election campaign.

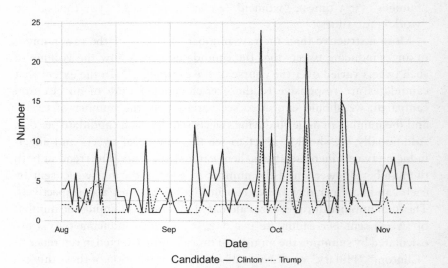

FIGURE 2.4. Donald Trump's and Hillary Clinton's anger-inducing tweet volume by day. This figure shows the number of anger-inducing tweets sent by Donald Trump and Hillary Clinton by day over the course of the general election campaign.

Unsurprisingly, both Donald Trump and Hillary Clinton sent more tweets and more tweets meant to elicit anger later into the campaign cycle. However, a closer analysis suggests that this pattern is not simply a trend of increasing tweets over time. On the contrary, both Trump and Clinton appear to be strategically responding to campaign events. For example, Hillary Clinton's most voluminous day of tweeting was October 20, 2016, the day after the third debate of the presidential cycle. On this day, Clinton's Twitter account retweeted other tweets that suggested Trump was full of "political cynicism," mocked his inexperience, or argued that he lacked an appropriate amount of civility. Clinton herself tweeted about Trump's bent toward mendacity, claiming that he lied 137 times over the course of the three presidential debates. She also tweeted her belief that Trump's behavior and policy views were "horrifying" and "part of a pattern."

Similarly, Donald Trump also sent his greatest amount of daily tweets on October 20, 2016. Much like Clinton was attempting to arouse anger toward Trump in order to cast her collective debate performances in the best possible light, Trump took to Twitter to agitate his base against Clinton at the conclusion of the debate cycle. On this day, Trump's Twitter account attacked Clinton's personal character on multiple fronts. In one tweet, Trump claimed that "Crooked Hillary took millions [of dollars in campaign donations] from oppressive [Middle Eastern] countries" and asked whether she would return these alleged donations. As if to drive home his attempt to impugn her character and elicit anger toward Clinton, Trump's tweet answered his own question: "Probably not." In a subsequent tweet, Trump claimed that, in office, Clinton "will use American tax dollars to provide amnesty for thousands of illegals." A few messages later, Trump claimed that "Crooked Hillary Clinton's foundation is a criminal enterprise." Trump also slammed Clinton over jobs ("she has never created a job in her life"), ties to Wall Street ("nothing more than a Wall Street puppet!"), and vacuousness ("she'll say anything and change nothing!"). Thus, Trump, like Clinton, was strategically stoking anger among his supporters at key junctures during the course of the presidential campaign.

2.4 ANGER AND PARTISAN MEDIA

In addition to examining the ways in which candidates themselves seek to elicit anger among their supporters, it is important to understand the ways in which various media outlets attempt to direct anger toward the two political parties and their associated candidates. Though media outlets are distinct from candidates and political parties, the contemporary era is one in which these distinctions are quickly fading. As Rosenfeld (2018) notes in his analysis of the development of the modern political parties, "[t]he relationship between the formal parties and their core group allies [have come] to be institutionalized and routinized." Expanding beyond organizational groups such as unions on the political left and the "Christian coalition" on the political right, these core groups have now come to include "media infrastructure in print, radio and television airwaves, and ...the Internet."

This increasing alignment between the Democratic and Republican parties and their media allies allows for a straightforward placement of the major cable TV channels along a left-right ideological spectrum. Fox News, in particular, tends to lean toward the political right, while MSNBC offers a left-leaning counterpart. These political leanings, combined with the fact that Americans are increasingly consuming national news at the expense of more locally focused media outlets (Hopkins 2018), suggests that these TV networks potentially have a large and increasingly important role in engendering anger within the electorate.

Such an expectation comports with the existing body of scholarship on the effects of a partisan media landscape on individual-level political behavior. DellaVigna and Kaplan (2007), for instance, show that the staggered introduction of Fox News to cable markets throughout the country precipitated an increase in the Republican share of the two-party vote in elections at both presidential and subpresidential levels. This increase, they claim, was through the twin mechanisms of political mobilization and persuasion.[16]

Drawing on Nielsen viewership ratings and leveraging Fox News' channel position within a TV package as an instrumental variable, Martin and Yurukoglu (2017) similarly illustrate how the consumption of Fox News has a powerful effect on voter behavior. These authors find that "Fox News increases Republican vote shares by 0.3 points among viewers induced into watching 2.5 additional minutes per week by variation in [channel] position." To further illustrate the dramatic effect that Fox News has had on Republican vote shares,

---

[16] Note, however, that more recent work suggests that media outlets do little to change political beliefs. On the contrary, media outlets tend to act as "echo chambers" that individuals self-select into (Arceneaux and Johnson 2013).

Martin and Yurukoglu (2017) show that removing Fox News from a channel lineup would have reduced the Republican share of the two-party presidential vote in the 2000 election by .46 percentage points; removing Fox News in 2004 would have led to a 3.59 percentage point drop in the Republican presidential vote share, and removing Fox News in 2008 would have led to a 6.34 percentage point drop.

To the extent that ideologically motivated TV channels can affect voter behavior and public opinion, it is likely that a portion of this effect is via the mechanism of increasing anger among viewers toward the opposing party and its candidates. Accordingly, we should expect to see shows airing on Fox News attempting to arouse anger toward the Democratic Party and its candidates for elected office. Likewise, we should expect that MSNBC's shows, particularly in more recent years as the channel has established itself as a liberal counterweight to Fox, purposely seek to elicit anger toward the Republican Party and its candidates.

To examine whether Fox News and MSNBC seek to elicit anger toward the Democratic and Republican Party, respectively, I analyze broadcast transcripts of nearly every show that has aired on both of these channels. These transcripts were downloaded via NewsBank. The list of shows covered, as well as the years for which transcripts are available, are shown in Table 2.2. Coverage begins in 1999 for the earliest shows and, for all shows, ends at the latest in 2016. Twelve shows in the data aired on Fox News and seventeen aired on MSNBC.

As with the analysis of Donald Trump's and Hillary Clinton's Twitter accounts, I consider shows to be attempting to elicit anger among their viewers if they spend a considerable amount of time discussing the opposing political party. Thus, for Fox News, shows will be considered as attempting to stoke anger if they mention Democrats, liberals, or Democratic candidates more than they mention Republicans, conservatives, or Republican candidates. Likewise, shows that aired on MSNBC will be classified as attempting to elicit anger if they mention Republicans, conservatives, or Republican candidates more than they mention Democrats, liberals, or Democratic candidates. While I expect Fox and MSNBC to talk about the opposing party more than the in-party, I further expect the degree to which shows on these two channels talk about the opposing party to be dependent on the political era in which the shows are airing. Specifically, I expect that the gap between out-party and in-party discussion will be bigger when the opposing party controls the White House.

TABLE 2.2 *Broadcast TV transcripts*

Show	Years Available
Fox News	
Fox News Edge	2001
Fox News Sunday	2001–2016
Glenn Beck	2009–2011
Hannity / Hannity & Colmes	1999–2016
O'Reilly Factor	1999–2016
On the Record	2002–2016
Special Report w/ Bret Baier	2009–2016
Special Report w/ Brit Hume	1999–2008
The Edge w/ Paula Zahn	1999–2001
The Five	2012–2013
The Kelly File	2013–2016
Your World w/ Neil Cavuto	1999–2016
MSNBC	
All In w/ Chris Hayes	2013–2016
Ashleigh Banfield on Location	2002
Buchanan & Press	2002–2003
Countdown w/ Keith Olbermann	2003–2011
Donahue	2002–2003
Hardball w/ Chris Matthews	1999–2016
Live w/ Dan Abrams	2007–2008
Morning Joe	2007–2013
Politics Nation	2011–2016
Rita Cosby Live & Direct	2005–2006
Scarborough Country	2003–2007
The Ed Show	2009–2013
The Last Word w/ Lawrence O'Donnell	2010–2016
The News w/ Brian Williams	1999–2002
The Rachel Maddow Show	2008–2016
The Savage Nation	2003
Tucker	2005–2008

This table shows the TV shows analyzed as well as the year coverage available for each show.

As discussed in Section 2.3 when discussing the nature of candidates' tweets, classifying anger-inducing speech by counting the number of times that candidates or parties are mentioned entails a set of trade-offs. In this context, Fox and MSNBC shows will be considered anger-inducing when they more frequently discuss the opposing political party and its candidates. On the one hand, such an approach is empirically straightforward. On the other hand, counting the number of times each show on Fox or

MSNBC discusses the two parties (or liberals and conservatives) does little to *prove* that they are doing so with the specific intent of stoking anger among their viewers.

However, the incentive structure governing the contemporary media environment suggests that mentions of the opposing political party and its candidates is most likely done within a negative context. Americans are generally not persuaded by partisan media but, rather, self-select into watching media sources that offer an ideological point of view with which they already agree (Arceneaux and Johnson 2013). Therefore, media outlets have an ever-present incentive to cater to the ideological tastes of their audience in order to maintain their market share. In this case, this implies that Fox News has an incentive to speak negatively of Democrats and Democratic candidates, while MSNBC has an incentive to speak negatively of Republicans and Republican candidates.

To begin, I first examine the most frequently used words on shows airing on Fox News and MSNBC. Word searches are limited to words that deal with politics or political affairs, such as "Democrat," "Republican," "President," "conservative," "liberal," "deficit," "taxes," and so on. In total, there are eighty-eight "political words," the full list of which can be found in the Appendix. I perform this calculation by examining the most used word by each show in each year. This produces a list of 116 words (one for each show-year in the data) for Fox News and 88 for MSNBC.

Across the entire timespan of shows that aired on Fox News, "Obama" was most frequently the most used word by show-year. Of the 116 show-years in the Fox News data, "Obama" was the most mentioned word 32 times (this translates to nearly 28% of the cases). "Bush" and "Trump" were the second and third most common, respectively, with "Bush" being the most used word 16 times and "Trump" being the most used word 13 times. These words were followed by "Iraq" (9 times), "Democrat" (6 times), and "Clinton" (6 times).[17] By contrast, "Republican" was the modal word in the MSNBC show-year dataset; this was the most common word for twenty-nine of the eighty-eight show-year observations in the data (33% of the observations). "Bush" was the second

---

[17] The emergence of Donald Trump onto the American political scene changed the nature of discourse on Fox News. Prior to Trump's run for the presidency, Fox spent considerably more time discussing Hillary Clinton, specifically, and Democratic candidates, more generally. When Trump became a candidate for President, Fox shifted their discussion toward him.

TABLE 2.3 *Top words on Fox News and MSNBC*

	Count		% of Total	
Word	Fox	MSNBC	Fox	MSNBC
America	4	2	3.4	2.3
Bush	16	13	13.8	14.8
Clinton	6	1	5.2	1.1
Democrat	6	2	5.2	2.3
Iraq	9	5	7.8	5.7
Obama	32	8	27.6	9.1
Republican	8	29	6.9	32.3
Tax	4	2	3.4	2.3
Trump	13	6	11.2	6.8
War	6	9	5.2	10.2

This table shows the number and percentage of time that each of the above words was the most frequently used word in a given show-year on Fox News and MSNBC.

most common word on MSNBC by show-year (13 times), followed by "Obama" (8 times), "Trump" (6 times), and "Romney" (6 times). The top ten words used between the two channels are shown in Table 2.3.

The pattern in these aggregate word counts suggests that the media is seeking to elicit anger among the public toward the opposing political party. For instance, "Obama" was four times as prevalent among the Fox News show-year data than in the MSNBC show-year data. Moreover, "Democrat" appears three times as often in the Fox News show-year data than the MSNBC show-year data. On the other hand, "Republican" was nearly 3.5 times as prevalent among the MSNBC show-year data than in the Fox News show-year data. MSNBC was also less likely to mention "Clinton" (in reference to either Bill or Hillary) than Fox News: "Clinton" was the most frequently used word in the MSNBC show-year data one-sixth as often as in the Fox News show-year data.

In addition to examining the overall channel-level patterns in word usage, understanding the patterns of word usage on specific shows helps to further illustrate the ways in which the media elicits anger within the electorate. To this end, I employ the same analysis as before but restrict the sample to the shows that aired during primetime slots. Here, "primetime" is defined as shows that begin airing at 7 PM on the East Coast. For Fox News, the list of shows that air or aired in primetime includes *Hannity* (as well as the show's precursor, *Hannity & Colmes*), *The Kelly File*, *The O'Reilly Factor*, and *On the Record with Greta Van Susteren*. For

MSNBC, *Hardball with Chris Matthews*, *All In with Chris Hayes*, *The Rachel Maddow Show*, *Countdown with Keith Olbermann*, and *The Last Word with Lawrence O'Donnell* comprise the list of shows that air or aired in primetime.

Restricting the sample to shows that air or aired in primetime yields fifty-five show-year observations for Fox News and forty-seven show-year observations for MSNBC. Among the Fox News primetime shows, "Obama" was the modal word by show-year, being the most frequent word used in the primetime show-year data 21 out of 55 times. Collectively, "Obama," "Clinton," and "Democrat" were the most used words 47% of the time in the Fox primetime show-year data. In the show-year data comprising all of the Fox News shows, these three words combined to be the most frequently used words 38% of the time. Among the non-primetime shows on Fox News, these words were the most frequently used in 28% of the show-years. This indicates a 24% increase in the use of "Obama," "Clinton," and "Democrat" among the primetime shows compared to the entire lineup and a staggering 68% increase compared to the non-primetime shows. Thus, among Fox News, it appears as if the trend toward eliciting anger toward the opposing political party is most pronounced among shows that air or previously aired in primetime.

As with the patterns displayed in the Fox News primetime data, shows that air or have aired in primetime on MSNBC appear to be more deliberately stoking anger among their viewers. Of the forty-seven show-year observations among the primetime MSNBC data, "Republican" was the most used word (20 times). "Bush" was the second most used word in the MSNBC primetime data (6 times), followed by "Obama" at 5. Collectively, "Republican," "Bush," and "Trump" were the most used words in the MSNBC show-year data 29 times. This comprises 62% of the data. These words collectively make up just under 55% of the most used words in the entire sample of MSNBC show-years and 43% in the sample of non-primetime shows. Thus, as with the Fox News data, shows that air or have aired in primetime on MSNBC appear to be eliciting anger more frequently. Compared to the entire sample, the primetime shows on MSNBC had "Republican," "Bush," or "Trump" as their most frequently used word by show-year 13% more often. Compared to the non-primetime sample, MSNBC primetime shows had one of these three words as their most used word 44% more often.

Just as important as the number of times Fox News and MSNBC mention the out-party or its candidates is the degree to which these channels mention the out-party and its candidates relative to their mentions of the in-party and the in-party's candidates. To assess the balance in terms of coverage within each of these networks, I divided the raw number of out-party mentions by the number of in-party mentions to obtain a *partisan balance ratio*. Thus, values above one indicate a higher amount of discussion about the out-party and its candidates relative to the in-party and its candidates. For Fox News, this indicates a higher prevalence of discussion about the Democratic Party and its candidates vis-à-vis the Republican Party and its candidates; for MSNBC, this indicates greater discussion of the Republican Party and its candidates compared to the Democratic Party and its candidates. Out-party and in-party mentions are counted among the set of words that includes "Democrat," "Republican," and previous candidates for the presidency: Bush, Clinton (which captures mentions of both Hillary and Bill), Obama, Romney, and Trump.[18]

The average partisan balance ratio for the entire show-year Fox News data is 1.21. The measure ranges from a low of .25 (*On the Record with Greta Van Susteren* in 2007) to a high of 4.7 (*The O'Reilly Factor* in 2008). These numbers suggest that, though there is variance in the data, shows that air or have aired on Fox News tend to mention the out-party and its candidates (Democrats) approximately 21% more often than the in-party and its candidates (Republicans).

The patterns in the MSNBC show-year data look similar. The mean partisan balance ratio among MSNBC shows is 1.47, indicating that, on average, MSNBC shows mention the out-party and its candidates (Republicans) 47% more often than the in-party and its candidates (Democrats). However, just like the Fox News data, there is considerable variance in the partisan balance ratio for MSNBC shows. The minimum value is .21 (*Live with Dan Abrams* in 2008) and the maximum value is 4.1 (*Rita Cosby Live & Direct* in 2006). A complete breakdown of the partisan balance ratio by show is shown in Table 2.4.

Interestingly, the average partisan balance ratio for both Fox News and MSNBC shifts considerably throughout the course of the time series. The overall trends in the mean partisan balance ratio by channel is shown in Figure 2.5. The trend lines in Figure 2.5 reveal a few important patterns.

---

[18] Using these candidates' mentions on Fox News and MSNBC gives a wide range of coverage in terms of discussion about presidential candidates. This list includes the previous two presidents from each party, as well as the most recent runner-up from each party.

TABLE 2.4 *Partisan balance ratio*

Show	Partisan Balance Ratio
Fox News	
Fox News Edge	.482
Fox News Sunday	1.06
Glenn Beck	2.28
Hannity / Hannity & Colmes	1.40
O'Reilly Factor	1.54
On the Record	1.14
Special Report w/ Bret Baier	1.57
Special Report w/ Brit Hume	.965
The Edge w/ Paula Zahn	.774
The Five	1.69
The Kelly File	1.15
Your World w/ Neil Cavuto	.730
MSNBC	
All In w/ Chris Hayes	1.42
Ashleigh Banfield on Location	2.93
Buchanan & Press	1.47
Countdown w/ Keith Olbermann	1.54
Donahue	1.95
Hardball w/ Chris Matthews	1.25
Live w/ Dan Abrams	.700
Morning Joe	1.34
Politics Nation	1.53
Rita Cosby Live & Direct	3.74
Scarborough Country	1.46
The Ed Show	1.23
The Last Word w/ Lawrence O'Donnell	1.57
The News w/ Brian Williams	1.80
The Rachel Maddow Show	1.53
The Savage Nation	1.05
Tucker	.890

This table shows the partisan balance ratio for each Fox News and MSNBC show.

First, it appears as if Fox News and MSNBC tend to have a greater imbalance in terms of out-party and in-party mentions during election years in which their preferred party is out of power. MSNBC, for instance, sees spikes in its mean partisan balance ratio in 2000, 2002, 2004, and 2006 – all years in which Republicans either won or had control of the White House. Relatedly, Fox News sees jumps in its mean partisan balance ratio in 2008 and 2014. Though there is less of a distinct pattern for Fox News

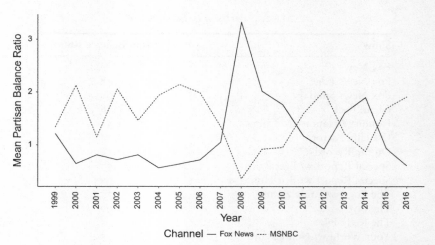

FIGURE 2.5. Average partisan balance ratio by channel. This figure shows the average partisan balance ratio for Fox News and MSNBC from 1999 to 2016.

(the mean partisan balance ratio decreases in the 2010 and 2016 elections) the overall pattern is indicative of partisan media elites engaging in more discussion of the out-party during election years.

In addition to this pattern, perhaps the most notable aspect of Figure 2.5 is the large jump in the partisan balance ratio on Fox News between 2007 and 2008. In 2007, Fox News' partisan balance ratio was 1.05; by 2008 it had jumped to 3.32. This 216% increase in the average partisan balance ratio was likely a result of Barack Obama's emergence onto the political scene, as well as his defeat of John McCain in that year's presidential election. As a charismatic politician who captured the interest of the nation en route to becoming the first African American President, Obama received a tremendous amount of media coverage by news stations of all political leanings. This "Obama effect" receives further support from the fact that MSNBC's partisan balance ratio in 2008 was its lowest in the entire time series because they, too, were disproportionately discussing Obama and his candidacy.

A similar pattern emerges in 2016. Rather than seeing a spike in the mean partisan ratio for both Fox News and MSNBC, the data suggests that, relative to the in-party, MSNBC is mentioning the out-party more while Fox News is mentioning the out-party less. Though this pattern is a mirror image to the pattern seen in 2008 the cause is likely the same. Just as in 2008, the 2016 presidential election saw the emergence of a unique candidate that dominated the airwaves across the ideological spectrum.

Indeed, Donald Trump's media coverage was so great that he accounted for 80% of CNN's August coverage of the Republican presidential campaign (Flint and Ballhaus 2015). Thus, just as was the case with Obama in 2008, the diverging trends in the mean partisan balance ratio between Fox News and MSNBC are indicative of a "Trump effect," whereby Trump's unique candidacy and astonishing victory in the presidential election saturated the airwaves across both of these channels.

2.5 CONCLUSION

In this chapter I sought to answer the question of whether political elites strategically elicit anger within the electorate. Using two comprehensive sources of data, one containing Tweets sent by every 2016 presidential candidate and the other containing transcripts of nearly every show that aired on Fox News and MSNBC between 1999 and 2016, the results presented in this chapter suggest that political elites are deliberately attempting to arouse anger among their co-partisans in the electorate. Moreover, the analyses here indicate that there is a periodicity to this trend. Rather than uniformly seeking to elicit anger across time, political elites appear to be increasing their anger-inducing rhetoric around salient campaign events such as elections and debates. Political elites in the news media appear to increase their anger-inducing rhetoric when the opposing political party is in power.

The reasoning behind elites' deliberate elicitation of anger has to deal with the nature of being a candidate for political office. As discussed in Section 2.2, politicians are increasingly engaging in what Grimmer (2013) calls "partisan taunting." Such taunting and vitriolic speech signals one's membership in the partisan group and solidifies electoral support. This chapter, then, supports Grimmer's (2013) theory of modern partisan discourse by showing the extent to which such anger-inducing rhetoric actually occurs.

In the next chapter I start to unpack the consequences of this anger for public opinion. Particularly, I examine the relationship between anger and citizens' trust in government. I begin this pursuit in Chapter 3 by showing how higher levels of trait-based anger are associated with lower levels of trust in government across various metrics; moreover, I show how this relationship is moderated by one's partisan affiliation. Chapter 4 then illustrates the causal relationship between anger and low levels of trust in government.

2.6 APPENDIX

The following words are used to analyze the topics of discussion on shows airing on Fox News and MSNBC in Section 2.4.

List of Political Words

1. Deficit
2. Regulation
3. Black
4. White
5. Hispanic
6. Asian
7. Female
8. Male
9. Men
10. Women
11. War
12. Labor
13. Union
14. Trade
15. Worker
16. Freedom
17. Patriotism
18. Patriot
19. Liberty
20. Jewish
21. Christian
22. Muslim
23. City
24. Cities
25. Cyber
26. Oil
27. Internet
28. Energy
29. Renewable
30. Financial
31. School
32. Education
33. Insurance

34. Tax
35. Jobs
36. Health care
37. President
38. Bush
39. McCain
40. Romney
41. Obama
42. Clinton
43. Politics
44. Politician
45. Party
46. Democrat
47. Republican
48. Left
49. Right
50. Ideology
51. Nuclear
52. Manufacturing
53. Israel
54. Iraq
55. Iran
56. Afghanistan
57. Middle East
58. Crisis
59. Government
60. Free
61. Market
62. Free market
63. Cost
64. Reform
65. Repeal
66. Bill

67. Filibuster
68. Pass
69. Security
70. Congress
71. White House
72. Capitol
73. Capitol Hill
74. The Hill
75. Americans
76. America
77. United States

78. USA
79. Administration
80. Governor
81. Gay
82. Lesbian
83. Homosexual
84. Heterosexual
85. Liberal
86. Conservative
87. Moderate
88. Trump

3

Trait-Based Anger and Governmental Distrust

> How much more grievous are the consequences of anger than the causes of it.
>
> — Marcus Aurelius

American politics in the contemporary era is defined by a new style of partisanship. Unlike their counterparts in the twentieth century, Americans today have an intense dislike of the opposing political party, its supporters, and its governing elite (Abramowitz and Webster 2016; Iyengar, Sood, and Lelkes 2012; Malka and Lelkes 2010; Mason 2013, 2015). This growth in negative partisanship and affective polarization has led to an electorate that is increasingly motivated by feelings of anger (see, e.g., Brader, Valentino, and Suhay 2008; Valentino et al. 2011). The consequences of this growing anger and partisan antipathy are clear: Americans are increasingly biased against the out-party (Iyengar and Westwood 2015), which has led to higher levels of political participation (Huddy, Mason, and Aarøe 2015) and straight-ticket voting (Jacobson 2015).

Yet, while scholars have spent a considerable amount of time examining the role of anger as an *emotion* in predicting patterns of political behavior and public opinion, the existing literature is devoid of studies examining how individuals whose *personality* predisposes them to be angry engage with the political world. This omission in the literature is surprising, especially as the burgeoning field of personality and politics suggests that there are characteristics innate to each individual that shape how he or she views politics and political affairs. These personality traits are predictive of phenomena as diverse as voting behavior, political engagement, and the size of interpersonal discussion networks (Gerber et al. 2010, 2012; Mondak 2010; Mondak and Halperin 2008).[1] In this chapter, I fill this gap in the extant literature by focusing on the role of trait-based anger in shaping citizens' views of the national government. I do this by utilizing the NEO-PI-R measure of an individual's trait-based level of anger, derived from clinical psychology, to show that higher levels of anger are associated with lower evaluations of the national government across a variety of metrics.

To begin, I briefly explicate the relationship between trait-based and state-based anger. I argue that the former is best conceptualized as a personality trait while the latter is best thought of as an emotion. I also argue that, while trait-based anger governs an individual's average disposition to be angry, emotional arousals can temporarily shift one's level of anger above or below their personality-governed level. Next, I develop a theory linking personality-governed anger to trust in the national government. I then introduce the data for this analysis and explain the relationship between the NEO-PI-R measure of anger and the more commonly used Big Five framework of personality. I then present a series of results linking higher levels of trait-based anger to lower levels of trust in government before concluding.

3.1 TRAIT-BASED VERSUS STATE-BASED ANGER

Anger, like all emotions, can be conceptualized as both an *emotion* and a *personality trait*. The former is best understood as something ephemeral that rises and falls according to various stimuli one experiences throughout the course of a day, week, or month. The latter, by contrast, is something more permanent that is less susceptible to change and daily fluctuations. Put differently, anger measured as a personality trait captures the extent to which an individual, on average, is angry or pacific (one's trait-based anger). Anger as an emotion, on the other hand, can best be thought of as a temporary deviation from an individual's personality-governed level of anger (one's state-based anger).

To further clarify the differences between emotions and personality traits, consider the graphic in Figure 3.1. This figure plots the distribution of a hypothetical individual's personality-governed level of anger. As can

---

[1] These studies all rely on the "Big Five" framework of personality.

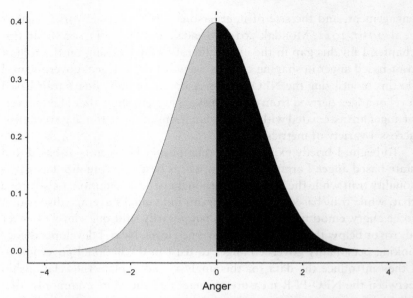

FIGURE 3.1. Hypothetical distribution of trait-based anger. This figure shows a hypothetical distribution of trait-based anger. The black shaded area indicates higher levels of anger and the gray shaded area indicates lower levels of anger.

be seen, the distribution is normal with mean zero.[2] Thus, on average, the individual who is depicted by this figure scores in the middle of the distribution of personality-governed levels of anger. However, just because this individual is particularly even-keeled in her temperament, it does *not* mean that she is insusceptible to temporary deviations in her personality distribution. Consider, for instance, the following scenarios. In the first scenario, imagine that the woman depicted by this personality profile is involved in a car wreck on her way home from work. The experience of the car wreck acts as a stimulus that prompts her to exhibit higher levels of anger. Thus, her level of anger would shift into the black area as she became angrier. On the other hand, this same individual could learn that she is being given a bonus for performing well at her job and may accordingly become less angry toward her boss or coworkers. In this scenario, her level of anger would shift into the gray region as she became less angry.

---

[2] Note that the numbers on this figure are for illustrative purposes only and do not have an empirical meaning.

The distinction between anger as an emotion and anger as a personality trait is more than just an exercise in conceptualization. Indeed, the most popular framework through which political scientists study emotions and politics, Affective Intelligence, argues that emotions are best understood within a trait-based context (Marcus, Neuman, and MacKuen 2000). From the theoretical notion of Affective Intelligence, then, scholars have largely focused on the *surveillance system*, which analyzes emotions, to the exclusion of the *disposition system*, which is more concerned with trait-based measures of personality. In this chapter, I draw on the role of the disposition system within Affective Intelligence to show how higher levels of trait-based anger are associated with lower levels of trust in government. More broadly, the argument laid out in this chapter suggests that Marcus, Neuman, and MacKuen's (2000) notion of Affective Intelligence is correct in positing that "emotions that become attached to politics ...have both state and trait characteristics."

3.2 ANGER, POLITICAL PREFERENCES, AND PUBLIC OPINION

Social psychologists have long recognized the role of personality and emotions in explaining patterns of behavior. In particular, anger has been found to be associated with myriad behavioral acts. Among other things, anger has been shown to affect social perception (Keltner, Ellsworth, and Edwards 1993), increase the use of group stereotypes and other heuristics (Bodenhausen, Sheppard, and Kramer 1994), prompt individuals to engage in risk-seeking activities (Lerner and Keltner 2001), and make individuals more punitive (Lerner and Tiedens 2006). Moreover, anger has been linked to higher levels of aggression and a lack of self-reflection (Tiedens 2001).

Though anger has been shown to alter various patterns of behavior and thought, how might it relate to individuals' evaluations of the national government? My argument draws from the psychological theories of Affective Intelligence (Marcus, Neuman, and MacKuen 2000) and "mood congruity" (Bower 1991). Affective Intelligence argues that reason and affect are not separate mental processes but, rather, are interconnected in a manner whereby affect influences when and how individuals think about various stimuli.

More specifically, Affective Intelligence argues that two different systems guide an individual's emotions. The first, the disposition system, regulates habits and general individual-level tendencies. As its name suggests, it governs one's overall disposition toward the social and political world. These habits and dispositions, Marcus, Neuman, and MacKuen (2000) claim, "behave very much like personality traits." Accordingly, the disposition system is best represented by the entire distribution in Figure 3.1. It is the cognitive function that determines the average, or habitual, pattern of emotional responses that one displays.

In contrast to the relative stability of the disposition system, the surveillance system deals with ephemera. It reacts to what can best be described as "shocks" to the personality tendencies of the disposition system. Marcus, Neuman, and MacKuen (2000) illustrate the function of the surveillance system by describing early human beings hearing the roar of a lion in a jungle. The lion's roar acts as a stimulus that momentarily heightens the anxiety of those who hear it. This emotional stimulus then leads to an action or set of actions (in this case, running away). Such an emotional reaction occurs within individuals regardless of their disposition toward being anxiety-prone or calm. Though the anxiety caused by the roar will eventually subside, the surveillance system has already done its job. In the context of Figure 3.1, the surveillance system is responsible for the temporary drifts into the gray or black zones.

Key for the theory linking higher levels of trait-based anger to lower levels of trust in government is the role of the disposition system in governing individual habits and patterns. To the extent that one's baseline personality can be conceptualized as a habit, then those individuals with higher levels of trait-based anger are habitually angry. Such habits and dispositions shape patterns of opinion and perception in predictable ways.

According to the theory of "mood congruity" (Bower 1991), people tend to evaluate objects, events, or scenarios in ways that are congruent with how they feel. Moreover, every personality trait and emotion has either a positive or a negative valence attached to it. Therefore, when an individual experiences an emotion with a positive valence – such as happiness or joy – they will evaluate objects positively. Conversely, when one experiences an emotion with a negative valence – such as anger – they will evaluate objects negatively. Because individuals with higher levels of trait-based anger are, by definition, more prone to habitual anger, they should be more likely to have consistently negative evaluations of the government than their more pacific counterparts.

While I expect those individuals with high levels of trait-based anger to have lower levels of trust in the government, it is also likely that the relationship between trait-based anger and trust in government is moderated by partisanship. As the theory of Affective Intelligence dictates, what makes people experience a given feeling or emotion "depends on the habits they have acquired." In terms of political beliefs, it is likely that Democrats and Republicans have acquired vastly different political habits. More specifically, Republicans tend to be more distrustful of the government (Hetherington 2005) while Democrats prefer to use government as a vehicle for social change. These partisan differences, combined with the ways in which anger should lower trust in government as described above, imply that the relationship between higher levels of trait-based anger and lower levels of trust in government should be stronger for Republicans.

3.3 PERSONALITY IN CONTEXT

While the theory I have outlined thus far suggests that higher levels of trait-based anger should be associated with lower evaluations of the national government, it is unlikely that an individual's personality is something that can vary over time. Indeed, according to the psychological literature from which it is derived, "personality" refers to a relatively stable set of characteristics that guide one's disposition toward the social world (Cobb-Clark and Schurer 2012; Digman 1989; McCrae and Costa 1994). Once formed, personality tends to change very little – if at all – barring major life events (McCrae and Costa 1994).

If this is the case, then why should we be interested in something that is predictive but does not vary over time? My argument is that, while personality does not vary over time, changing electoral and political contexts can make an individual's trait-based level of anger more or less salient for predicting and guiding patterns of political behavior. In particular, the current era is likely to be one where those individuals with high levels of trait-based anger should have distinct preferences and opinions about politics and government compared to their more pacific counterparts. This is not only due to increasing elite polarization, but also due to the dramatic increase in negative affect among partisans and between partisan and social groups. While Americans used to feel largely indifferent about the opposing political party and its supporters, negative affect has increased tremendously in recent years as racial, cultural, and ideological identities have become intertwined with partisan affiliation (Abramowitz and Webster 2016; Mason 2015). This anger-fueled negative affect and the political environment it has created now means that "partisanship elicits more extreme evaluations and behavioral responses to ingroups and outgroups" than longstanding cleavages such as race (Iyengar and Westwood 2015). Accordingly, understanding how anger shapes individuals' dispositions toward the political world in the contemporary era of high polarization is of tremendous importance.

3.4 STUDY DESIGN

The data for the analyses in this chapter are part of a larger survey on personality, emotions, and political behavior. Fielded via Survey Sampling International (SSI), the survey is a national sample of registered voters. The total sample size is 3,262 respondents. Of these, 42.8% are men and 57.2% are women; 82% are White, 6.6% are African-American, and 5.5% are Hispanic; finally, 85.4% have at least some college education and 14.6% have only a high school diploma.

The survey asked individuals to fill out a series of demographic questions, such as age, race, gender, education, and household income. Participants were also asked to disclose their partisan and ideological identification along a seven-point scale. In addition to demographic and partisan/ideological information, the survey asked participants a series of questions about participatory acts and candidate choice. Among other things, individuals were asked about their voting habits and future voting intentions, how frequently they talk to others about politics, whether they have made campaign donations, and whether they have attempted to influence someone else's vote choice.

Finally, individuals were asked a series of questions designed to measure their evaluations of the national government. These questions measure how much individuals believe the government is unresponsive to the concerns and interests of the public, and the belief that the government is corrupt and never serves the public interest. Both questions are measured on a 0–10 scale, where higher values indicate more negative evaluations of the government.

NEO-PI-R ANGRY HOSTILITY. The most important part of the survey is the set of questions that measure individuals' trait-based level of anger. While the majority of the personality and politics literature operationalizes "personality" by means of the Big Five framework (see, e.g., Cooper, Golden, and Socha 2013; Gerber et al. 2010; Mondak 2010; Mondak and Halperin 2008; Mondak et al. 2010), I jettison this measure in favor of Costa and McCrae's (1995) NEO-PI-R measure. Due to its careful and detailed measurement, the NEO-PI-R has become the "gold standard" in measuring individuals' personalities. However, its usage has been limited in academic settings because the full battery contains 240 questions. While such a length precludes using the NEO-PI-R to measure an individual's personality in most cases, because I am primarily interested here in an individual's personality-governed level of anger, only ten questions are needed. Thus, while using the entire NEO-PI-R survey battery is typically infeasible, relying on it to measure just one aspect of an individual's personality is not time intensive and does not present survey respondents with more of a burden than they are used to.

In order to measure how angry each individual is, participants were asked to fill out the questionnaire for the Angry Hostility NEO-PI-R facet-level trait.[3] According to the NEO Personality Inventory survey developed by Costa and McCrae (1995) to measure the Big Five, each of the five domains (e.g., openness to new experiences, conscientiousness) is comprised of six lower-level facets. Each of the facets "represent[s] the more closely covarying elements within the domain" and are mutually exclusive. Each domain contains six facets because, according to Costa and McCrae (1995), "inclusion of more than six would soon lead to intellectual overload." Furthermore, the factor analyses employed to identify the facets within each domain require a requisite amount of variables to facilitate replication (Gorsuch 1983). Though these facets do not cover the entirety of the variance within each domain, they do appear to capture a large amount while still remaining parsimonious. By aggregating each facet-level score within the five respective domains, Big Five scores can be obtained for any given individual.

The Angry Hostility facet-level trait is derived from the Emotional Stability domain of the Big Five, and it largely measures the degree to which an individual is temperamental in their behavior (Lord 2007). The Angry Hostility facet-level trait is measured by a series of ten statements, five of which are positively coded and five of which are reverse coded. Each statement is presented to an individual and then that individual is

[3] In actuality, the measure used here is slightly different from that found on the NEO-PI-R. Because the NEO-PI-R is a proprietary test of *Psychological Assessment Resources, Inc.* and its usage is prohibited in academic studies, psychologists have collaborated to create "open source" measures of numerous scales that correlated highly with their proprietary counterparts. Despite being slightly different measures, the "open source" version used here correlates highly with the actual NEO-PI-R test. Analyses have shown that the "open source" measure of the Angry Hostility facet-level trait has a remarkably high correlation, .90, with the NEO-PI-R measurement. For more information, see http://ipip.ori.org/newNEO_FacetsTable.htm or Goldberg et al. (2006).

asked to state their level of agreement or disagreement with the veracity of that statement with regard to their own life. Agreement is measured on a five-point scale ranging from one to five. A rating of one indicates that an individual "strongly disagrees" with a statement about herself, a rating of two indicates that an individual "disagrees" with that statement, a rating of three indicates that an individual is "neutral" about the statement, while ratings of four and five indicate that an individual "agrees" or "strongly agrees" with the statement, respectively. The final score for an individual's level of Angry Hostility is simply the summation of each of the ten questions. Formally, anger is measured as follows:

$$Anger = \sum_{i=1}^{5} x_i + \sum_{j=1}^{5} x_j \qquad (3.1)$$

where i is the positively coded statements and j is the reverse coded statements. The positively coded statements of the Angry Hostility facet-level scale are "I get angry easily," "I get irritated easily," "I get upset easily," "I am often in a bad mood," and "I tend to lose my temper." The reverse coded statements are "I rarely get irritated," "I seldom get mad," "I am not easily annoyed," "I keep my cool," and "I rarely complain." By asking questions that are positively and negatively coded, the survey instrument is less susceptible to being answered in socially desirable ways. The measure ranges from 10 to 50, with higher scores indicating higher levels of trait-based anger. Importantly, the ten items that comprise the scale have a high degree of inter-item reliability. Indeed, the Cronbach's alpha for the scale is a remarkably high .87.

Though use of the Angry Hostility facet-level trait seems like a reasonable way to gain theoretical leverage on questions of interest when compared to the domain-level characteristics of the Big Five, one reasonable concern is that these lower-level traits might lack predictive power. If this is the case, then taking such an approach might entail a trade-off between cogent theory building and analytical utility. Fortunately, this does not appear to be the case. Comparisons between the Big Five domain-level characteristics and the facet-level traits show that "a few carefully selected personality facet scales can predict as well as or better than can all of the Big Five factor scales combined." Moreover, this same analysis found that "a substantial part of the criterion variance predicted by the facet scales is variance not predicted by the [domain] scales" (Paunonen and Ashton 2001). Similarly, in their study of personality disorders, Reynolds and Clark (2001) find that the domain-level characteristics are too broad to generate "clinically meaningful descriptions" of disorders. Thus, their suggestion is to make use of the facet-level traits to obtain a "substantial increase in predictive power and descriptive resolution" on questions of interest (Reynolds and Clark 2001).

In addition to anger, I also include the NEO-PI-R measure of anxiety as a control variable in some of the model specifications. As with the NEO-PI-R measure of anger, the NEO-PI-R measure of anxiety is comprised of five positively coded statements and five reverse-coded statements.[4] And, as with the measure of anger, each individual's score on the NEO-PI-R measure of anxiety is a summation of these ten constituent terms. Scores range from 10 to 50 with higher scores indicating greater levels of trait-based anxiety.

Importantly, the NEO-PI-R measures of personality do not explicitly capture an individual's level of political anger (or anxiety). On the contrary, this measure of personality captures an individual's daily propensity to be angry (or anxious) at any interpersonal or social phenomena. Thus, the NEO-PI-R measure of personality is a general, rather than an explicitly political, instrument. The results presented in the next section, then, are best interpreted as an examination of the relationship between general personality-governed anger and trust in government.

3.5 ANGER AND EVALUATIONS OF THE NATIONAL GOVERNMENT

To estimate the relationship between trait-based anger and trust in government, I run models with the following functional form:

$$y_i = \alpha + \beta_1 \rho_i + \mathbf{X} + \epsilon \qquad (3.2)$$

where y_i captures individual i's level of trust in government, which, depending on the model, is operationalized as the individual's belief that the government is unresponsive to the concerns and interests of the public, or the belief that the national government is corrupt. As described in Section 3.4, higher scores on these measures indicate a greater belief that the government is unresponsive and corrupt. Individual i's score on the NEO-PI-R measure of trait-based anger is captured by ρ_i, while $\mathbf{X}$ is a

---

4 The positively coded statements are "I worry about things," "I fear for the worst," "I am afraid of many things," "I get stressed out easily," and "I get caught up in my problems." The reverse-coded statements are "I am not easily bothered by things," "I am relaxed most of the time," "I am not easily disturbed by events," "I don't worry about things that have already happened," and "I adapt easily to new situations."

vector of controls. Control variables include dummy variables for females and non-Whites; it also contains measures for partisanship (coded as -1 for Republicans, o for independents, and 1 for Democrats) and ideology (measured on the standard 7-point scale, where higher values indicate a more conservative ideology), income, and educational attainment. Some models also include a control variable for an individual's level of trait-based anxiety. Estimation is via ordinary least squares (OLS) regression.

The results of the regressions estimating the relationship between trait-based anger and trust in government are shown in Table 3.1. The results show that anger is predictive of negative evaluations of the national government across both metrics. Individuals with higher levels of trait-based anger are more likely to believe that the government is both unresponsive to the concerns and interests of the public, and that the government is

TABLE 3.1 *Anger and evaluations of government*

	Govt. Unresponsive		Govt. Corrupt	
	(1)	(2)	(3)	(4)
Anger	0.028***	0.022***	0.046***	0.039***
	(0.006)	(0.007)	(0.006)	(0.007)
Anxiety		0.010		0.013*
		(0.008)		(0.008)
Partisanship	−0.419***	−0.422***	−0.482***	−0.471***
	(0.060)	(0.061)	(0.061)	(0.062)
Female	−0.141	−0.168*	−0.075	−0.113
	(0.088)	(0.091)	(0.089)	(0.092)
Non-White	−0.071	−0.069	0.181	0.188
	(0.113)	(0.115)	(0.114)	(0.116)
Income	−0.044***	−0.044***	−0.050***	−0.046***
	(0.013)	(0.013)	(0.013)	(0.013)
Ideology	0.062**	0.066**	0.086***	0.092***
	(0.030)	(0.031)	(0.031)	(0.031)
Education	−0.137***	−0.132***	−0.182***	−0.184***
	(0.032)	(0.033)	(0.032)	(0.033)
Constant	6.844***	6.700***	6.234***	6.013***
	(0.245)	(0.268)	(0.248)	(0.272)
N	3,026	2,943	3,030	2,948
R^2	0.064	0.066	0.098	0.098

$^*p < .1; ^{**}p < .05; ^{***}p < .01.$
This table shows the relationship between trait-based anger and evaluations of the national government. Individuals who are predisposed to be angry have more negative views of the government across both metrics.

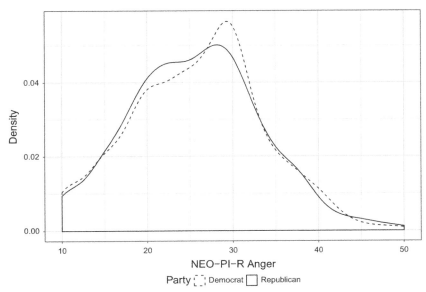

FIGURE 3.2. Distribution of anger by partisanship. This figure shows the distribution of scores on the NEO-PI-R measure of anger by partisan affiliation.

corrupt. The credibility of these results receives support from the fact that the model has a considerable degree of face validity; indeed, the model indicates that Democrats are less likely to have negative evaluations of the government than self-identifying independents and Republicans, while ideological conservatives are more likely than others to view the government negatively. The models presented in columns two and four indicate that the results are robust to the inclusion of measures of trait-based anxiety.

Though there appears to be a relationship between trait-based anger and trust in government, the theory outlined above predicts that the strength of this relationship should differ based on one's party identification. Before examining the ways in which the relationship between trait-based anger and trust in government might be conditional upon one's partisanship, it is useful to first examine the distribution of scores on the NEO-PI-R measure of trait-based anger by partisan affiliation. As shown in Figure 3.2, there is very little difference in the distribution of scores on the NEO-PI-R anger measure by party affiliation. While Democratic respondents have a higher modal score on the measure, the right tail is slightly fatter for Republican respondents. Thus, while

TABLE 3.2 *Anger and evaluations of government, with interaction term.*

	Govt. Unresponsive		Govt. Corrupt	
	(1)	(2)	(3)	(4)
Anger	0.026***	0.019***	0.043***	0.036***
	(0.006)	(0.007)	(0.006)	(0.007)
Partisanship	−0.806***	−0.814***	−1.000***	−1.015***
	(0.164)	(0.166)	(0.165)	(0.168)
Anger X Partisanship	0.015**	0.015**	0.020***	0.021***
	(0.006)	(0.006)	(0.006)	(0.006)
Anxiety		0.010		0.013*
		(0.008)		(0.008)
Female	−0.135	−0.162*	−0.067	−0.104
	(0.088)	(0.091)	(0.089)	(0.092)
Non-White	−0.064	−0.060	0.191*	0.200*
	(0.113)	(0.115)	(0.114)	(0.116)
Income	−0.043***	−0.044***	−0.050***	−0.045***
	(0.013)	(0.013)	(0.013)	(0.013)
Ideology	0.064**	0.068**	0.089***	0.095***
	(0.030)	(0.031)	(0.031)	(0.031)
Education	−0.135***	−0.130***	−0.179***	−0.181***
	(0.032)	(0.033)	(0.032)	(0.033)
Constant	6.875***	6.732***	6.276***	6.059***
	(0.245)	(0.268)	(0.248)	(0.271)
N	3,026	2,943	3,030	2,948
R^2	0.066	0.068	0.101	0.102

$*p < .1; **p < .05; ***p < .01.$
These results show how the relationship between trait-based anger and trust in government is conditional upon one's partisanship. Trait-based anger is more strongly related to lower levels of trust in government for Democrats.

Republicans have more individuals who are extremely angry, Democratic respondents are, on average, angrier than Republican respondents.

The lack of distinct distributions on the NEO-PI-R anger measure by partisanship casts doubt on the expectation that partisanship has the ability to moderate the relationship between trait-based anger and trust in government. However, to more definitively test this relationship, I re-ran the models as defined in Equation 3.2 except this time included an interaction term between the measure of trait-based anger and the trichotomous measure of partisanship. As before, some of the model specifications also include a control for an individual's level of trait-based anxiety. These results are presented in Table 3.2.

The results of the models displayed in Table 3.2 are somewhat surprising. The expectation was that Republicans' tendency to be distrustful of the government would lead to a stronger relationship between trait-based anger and trust in government for those who identify with the Republican Party. The results suggest that the opposite is true: the relationship between trait-based anger and trust in government is actually stronger for Democrats. One potential reason for this result is that being distrustful of the government is a key part of the Republican identity. Thus, there may simply be less room for anger to operate as a mechanism through which distrust may increase. Conversely, because Democrats often seek to use government as a vehicle to achieve various social goals, it is likely that they are more apt to trust the government than are Republicans. As a result, there is a greater opportunity for anger to shift evaluations of the government downward for Democrats than for Republicans. However, such an explanation for the findings in Table 3.2 is merely preliminary. More precisely understanding the nature of these results promises to be an exciting area for future research.

3.6 A NOTE ON THE CAUSAL ORDERING

Though the above results indicate that higher levels of anger are related to various forms of political behavior, it is not possible to say that having higher levels of trait-based anger *causes* individuals to behave differently than their more pacific counterparts. Indeed, one potential concern is that any sort of causal arrow goes the other way. That is, instead of anger affecting forms of political behavior and public opinion, it is possible that individuals are projecting their political beliefs and opinions onto personality self-reports. While the data do not allow for an adjudication between these two causal pathways, extant theory provides a useful guide as to how these results should best be interpreted.

According to the literature from which it is derived, personality is seen as a stable characteristic of individuals that is formed early in the course of life and, once it is formed, seldom – if ever – changes (Cobb-Clark and Schurer 2012; Digman 1989; McCrae and Costa 1994). As McCrae and Costa (1994) note, "the greatest part of the reliable variance (i.e., variance not due to measurement error) in personality traits is stable." These same authors also show that personality stability exists across gender and racial groups. If personality is stable and formed largely during the early stages of life, then it seems implausible to assume that individuals both learn about politics and its associated nuances *and* adopt certain policy preferences before their personality begins to develop. The more likely explanation is that personality development is temporally prior to the formation of issue preferences.

However, one further objection is that, even if personality is formed before the adoption of issue preferences, it is possible that individuals might alter the ways in which they respond to a personality battery precisely because of their issue positions. Moreover, respondents may simply misunderstand the personality questions or they may present "false answers" as a form of social desirability bias (though neither of these problems are limited to surveys that seek to measure personality traits). Fortunately, empirical analyses suggest that social desirability plays a minimal role in survey responses pertaining to personality measures. Citing numerous studies, Piedmont (1989) claims that "more direct and 'obvious' [survey] items possess better validity than subtle items" and that "when respondents are presented with a direct query about their internal state, they will give an honest and accurate response." Thus, concerns about social desirability bias in response to personality questions appear to be unfounded.

Finally, even if personality was not stable (and therefore was susceptible to changes given a survey battery) and/or individuals projected their issue positions onto survey batteries seeking to measure personality traits, such a problem is likely avoided here due to the way in which the survey was designed. Indeed, the questions measuring individuals' baseline level of anger on the NEO-PI-R scale was presented *before* the series of questions about issue positions. Accordingly, from a mechanical standpoint, it was impossible for respondents to this survey to answer their personality questions based on the way in which they answered questions about issue positions.

While causality cannot be determined given the nature of these data, theory and matters of research design suggest that the causal ordering flows from an individual's level of anger to patterns of political behavior and public opinion. Arguing that the causal arrow instead points in the other direction would require more assumptions – assumptions that are tenuous at best.

3.7 CONCLUSION AND DISCUSSION

In this chapter I have argued that higher levels of trait-based anger, as measured on the NEO-PI-R scale, shape patterns of public opinion. Specifically, I have argued that higher levels of trait-based anger shape public opinion by lowering individuals' trust in the national government across two metrics: the belief that the government is unresponsive to the concerns and interests of the public and that the government is corrupt. Moreover, I have shown that the degree to which higher levels of trait-based anger are associated with lower evaluations of the national government is conditional upon an individual's partisan identification. Indeed, the results in Table 3.2 indicate that trait-based anger is more effective in lowering trust in government for Democrats than Republicans.

Future work should more thoroughly examine the precise reasoning as to why anger is more efficacious in lowering trust in government among Democrats than Republicans. I have speculated that anger shapes Democrats' views of the government more than Republicans' because Republicans are generally already more distrustful of the government than Democrats. Because one of the central tenets of modern-day Democratic political philosophy is that government can and should be used for societal good, Democratic partisans are more apt to be trusting of the government. Thus, there is more room for anger to operate as a catalyst for increasing distrust among those on the political left than the political right. However, future studies should more rigorously test this claim to better understand the nature of the relationship between trait-based anger and trust in government.

Crucially, the findings presented in this chapter hinge upon the theoretical idea that, though an individual's personality tends to remain stable over time, changes in electoral and political contexts (such as a high degree of elite and/or mass polarization) can make certain personality traits more or less salient for guiding patterns of public opinion. Future work, then, should explore what sorts of factors can make personality traits – whether anger, anxiety, or something else – more or less salient within the political realm. Given the wide array of traits measured by the NEO-PI-R personality scale and the constantly shifting nature of political discourse, plenty of work remains for students of political behavior and political psychology.

4

The Causal Effect of Anger on Trust in Government

I'm as mad as hell, and I'm not gonna take this anymore!
— Howard Beale

In the previous chapter I argued that higher levels of trait-based anger are associated with lower evaluations of the national government. In doing so, I utilized the role of the disposition system in Affective Intelligence (AI) to show how habits and patterns can affect one's views toward political institutions. What the preceding analysis left unexamined is the role of *emotions* – those momentary perturbations that are governed by the surveillance system – in predicting degrees of trust in the government. Moreover, while the analysis in Chapter 3 showed a relationship between anger and low levels of trust in government, it is important to probe further to determine whether anger has a causal effect in reducing citizens' trust in government or whether it is simply correlational.[1]

In this chapter, I utilize an experimental design on a national sample of registered voters to show that anger has a causal effect in reducing trust in government. Importantly, I find that anger is able to affect an individual's views of the national government even when it is aroused through apolitical means. I also show that the angrier an individual is, the more distrust of the government they will express. This suggests that, in terms of anger's ability to lower trust in government, the magnitude of the anger is more important than the source of the anger. In total, the

---

[1] This chapter is based largely off of Webster (2018a). This chapter has been adapted by permission from Springer Nature.

results from this chapter suggest that anger plays a broad and powerful role in shaping how Americans view their governing institutions.

To begin, I outline a theory as to why both targeted political anger and generalized apolitical anger can affect Americans' trust in the national government. I then explicate an experimental research design that captures the causal effect of anger on trust in government. I then build on the results of this experiment to show that the magnitude, rather than the source, of an individual's anger is the most important element in predicting levels of distrust in the national government. After this, I utilize data from the American National Election Studies (ANES) to show that the results I obtain from my experimental analysis are replicable in a broader setting. I then conclude with a discussion on the implication of these results for the health of American government.

4.1 THE BEHAVIORAL EFFECTS OF ANGER

Canonical models of political behavior suggest that individuals are purely rational actors who are unaffected by emotions (see, e.g., Downs 1957). However, recent work has cogently shown that anger can and does play an important role in shaping political behavior and public opinion across a wide range of issue areas. Banks and Valentino (2012), for instance, show that anger causes a reduction in support for affirmative action policies and that this anger is at the root of symbolic racism and racial resentment. Relatedly, Banks (2014) shows that heightened levels of anger cause shifts in opinions on health care reform. Specifically, Banks's (2014) study shows that anger causes a reduction in support for health care reform among racial conservatives by triggering symbolic racism. Conversely, higher levels of anger serve to increase support for health care reform among those who are racially liberal. The mechanism through which these findings occur can largely be explained by MacKuen et al.'s (2010) argument that anger causes people to fall back on familiar information and preconceived ideas.

Additional studies have illustrated how anger serves to reduce levels of trust. For instance, Dunn and Schweitzer (2005) utilize an experimental design to show how higher levels of anger play a causal role in reducing an individual's level of interpersonal trust. Importantly, this effect is found through arousing an individual's level of "incidental anger." This implies that experiencing anger in one situation can affect a person's reactions in an unrelated setting. Applying their model to business dealings,

Dunn and Schweitzer (2005) show how experiencing anger in one meeting may cause a manager to also be angry "with a client in an unrelated setting."

Relatedly, Gino and Schweitzer (2008) find that angry individuals are less willing to accept advice from others. Similar to the mechanism found by Dunn and Schweitzer (2005), Gino and Schweitzer (2008) note that the reason that angry individuals are less willing to accept advice from others is because higher levels of anger serve to lower an individual's level of interpersonal trust. Much like the findings provided by Dunn and Schweitzer (2005), the results that Gino and Schweitzer (2008) present are also obtained by heightening levels of "incidental anger." Anger, then, has been shown to affect trust in broad and meaningful ways across multiple studies. If these findings about anger and trust exist at the individual level, then it makes sense to expect that we would see them at an institutional level as well. Examining how anger – both about politics and that which is apolitical – plays a similar role at such a level is the task to which I now turn.

4.2 ANGER, BEHAVIOR, AND TRUST IN GOVERNMENT

4.2.1 Targeted Political Anger and Trust in Government

That targeted political anger might be able to affect evaluations of the national government has a considerable amount of support from studies within political behavior and political psychology. In addition to being associated with higher levels of both "cheap" and "costly" forms of participation (see, e.g., Valentino et al. 2011), anger about politics has also been linked to internal political efficacy (Valentino, Gregorowicz, and Groenendyk 2009). As Valentino, Gregorowicz, and Groenendyk (2009) argue, policy threats – for instance, what a liberal voter might experience when a more conservative politician proposes privatizing Social Security – prompt individuals to become angry. Among those individuals who have high levels of internal political efficacy, this anger serves as a catalyst for engagement and participation in future elections.

Though these studies link anger to political participation and engagement, the mechanism they uncover is important for understanding how anger might affect attitudes toward the national government. In each case, anger is seen as a biological response to some upsetting, or otherwise unwanted, political stimuli. The result of this anger is some set of actions or thought processes against the source of the stimulus. Importantly, because "anger ...has an unusually strong ability to capture attention" and influence "perceptions, beliefs, ideas, reasoning, and ultimately choices" (Lerner and Tiedens 2006), the responses elicited from anger are oftentimes predictable. Crucially, anger typically elicits negative appraisals from individuals toward that which induced the anger – such as television reports (Kim and Cameron 2011), terrorists (Lerner et al. 2003), art (Silvia 2009), or companies (Bennett 1997).

Following this logic, individuals who are angry about politics or political affairs should have lower evaluations of the national government. As perhaps the most visible representation of politics and political affairs – especially in a climate of nationalized politics (Hopkins 2018) – the national government is a likely target for the negative appraisals that targeted political anger should elicit. Indeed, such a relationship between anger and lower levels of trust in government is especially likely to exist in the contemporary era. Because negative partisan affect in the electorate has grown considerably over the past few decades (Abramowitz and Webster 2016; Iyengar and Westwood 2015; Mason 2013, 2015), Americans are increasingly exposed to stimuli seeking to induce anger toward the opposing political party, its governing elite, and its supporters in the electorate. Whether these stimuli come from elite rhetoric (Layman and Carsey 2002), fellow partisans (Klar 2014), or partisan-friendly media outlets (Prior 2007), political discourse in the contemporary era is decisively negative in tone. Moreover, because these anger-inducing stimuli often encourage individuals to gauge the governmental performance of a particular party (see, e.g., Citrin 1974; Hetherington and Rudolph 2015), targeted political anger should cause individuals to have lower evaluations of the national government.

4.2.2 Generalized Apolitical Anger and Trust in Government

In addition to this targeted form of political anger described above, it is also possible for a more generalized type of anger that is aroused through apolitical means to affect an individual's evaluations of the national government. That generalized apolitical anger might be able to shape individuals' evaluations of the national government is due, in part, to the process of AI. Pioneered by Marcus, Neuman, and MacKuen (2000), AI "conceptualize[s] affect and reason not as oppositional but as complementary, as two functional mental faculties in a delicate, interactive, highly functional dynamic balance." The complementary and interactive nature of emotion and reason operates such that one's emotional reaction to a particular stimulus determines whether an individual will react to that stimulus by relying on old habits or by seeking new information. Moreover, AI claims that "affect also influences when and how we *think* about ...things" (Marcus, Neuman, and MacKuen 2000, emphasis in original).

Schwarz and Clore (1983) put forth a similar argument, claiming that emotion and reason are interconnected processes. Specifically, their argument is that affect plays a large role in individuals' processing and comprehension of information. In their seminal study, Schwarz and Clore (1983) experimentally induced either happy or sad emotions in subjects and then asked individuals to give subjective evaluations about their quality of life. The results they found suggest that happy individuals and sad individuals tend to have positive and negative evaluations about their quality of life, respectively. Much like Marcus, Neuman, and MacKuen's (2000) theory of AI, this implies that emotions and reason are intertwined in a manner where the former play a large role in influencing the latter. In other words, "one cannot think without feeling" (Marcus 2002).

How, then, should generalized apolitical anger be expected to lower individuals' views of the national government? As discussed above and previously in Chapter 3, insights from AI and the psychological theory of "mood-congruity" (Bower 1991) suggest that an individual's felt emotion shapes the ways in which he or she renders a judgment on any given thing. Extant research also suggests that anger is an emotion with a negative valence (Lerner and Keltner 2001; Moons, Eisenberger, and Taylor 2010). Accordingly, individuals who are primed to exhibit higher levels of anger will view the target of their anger in a negative light. Yet, the nature of emotions suggests that the negative evaluations that are produced by emotional outbursts of anger can – and oftentimes do – "spill over" to affect views of people, situations, or institutions that are orthogonal to the original source of an individual's anger.

The ability of emotions to "spill over" to other areas of one's life was cogently illustrated by Forgas and Moylan (1987), who surveyed moviegoers about various items (e.g., political judgments, expectations about the future) after they had seen a movie with a particular overall valence. They found that individuals who saw a movie that, overall, had a happy valence, tended to give optimistic judgments on survey batteries. By contrast, those individuals who saw movies that had an aggregate sad or aggressive valence were more pessimistic in their judgments.[2] In terms of political affairs, for instance, Forgas and Moylan (1987) found that individuals gave lower evaluations of national and local Australian politicians after seeing a sad or aggressive film. Additionally, moviegoers who saw a sad or aggressive film were less likely to believe that a nuclear war could be avoided and were more likely to believe that the state of the economy was poor. These findings lend credence to the theory of mood-congruity, and suggest that anger should "be expected to activate negative concepts, and ...negative judgments" (Bodenhausen, Sheppard, and Kramer 1994) across a wide range of possible issues.

Therefore, by eliciting generalized apolitical anger and then immediately asking individuals how they feel about the national government, the negative valence attached to the emotional outburst of anger is likely to "spill over" and shape individuals' evaluations of the government. Thus, although the mode through which the anger was elicited was apolitical, it is possible to subsequently channel that anger toward a political target and, via the mechanism of mood-congruity, lower evaluations of that political object.

Though both targeted political anger and generalized apolitical anger should affect individuals' evaluations of the national government, the effect sizes should not be equal. Instead, the magnitude of the targeted political anger effect should be larger than that of the effect for generalized apolitical anger. This is because, while the anger derived via apolitical means must "spill over" to political targets in order to have an effect, the targeted political anger is more direct. Because targeted political anger, by definition, directly elicits anger about politics and political affairs, the degree to which individuals negatively view the object that elicited the anger should be stronger.

4.3 ANGER, EVALUATIONS OF GOVERNMENT, AND CAUSALITY

To examine the causal effect of anger on citizens' trust in government, I utilize an experimental design embedded in a national survey to exogenously vary individuals' level of anger before measuring levels of trust in government. The data for this experiment come from a survey fielded

---

[2] Forgas and Moylan's (1987) movies with a happy valence were *Beverly Hills Cop, Police Academy 2, Back to the Future,* and *Brewster's Millions.* Their movies with a sad valence were *Dance with a Stranger, Mask, Birdy,* and *Killing Fields.* Their movies with an aggressive valence were *First Blood, Rambo, Mad Max 2,* and *Mad Max 3.*

in Fall 2016 via Survey Sampling International (SSI). The survey is a national – though not representative – sample of registered voters with a total sample size of 3,262 respondents. Approximately 57% of the respondents are female, 82% are White, and 85.4% have at least some college education.

In order to alter individuals' level of anger, I utilize a technique known as emotional recall.[3] This technique, which has been used widely in psychology (see, e.g., Lerner and Keltner 2001; Lerner et al. 2003), asks individuals to write a short paragraph about a time they felt a particular emotion. The idea of such a technique is that by recalling a specific time that they felt a given emotion, that individual will temporarily experience a heightened sense of that same emotion. For the purposes of this study, individuals were asked to recall a time that they felt "very angry about politics." They were then instructed to describe as precisely as possible how this experience made them feel. Individuals in the control group were asked to recall what they had for breakfast in the morning. This question provides a useful control group because it is benign in nature and is tangential to any emotional state.

One important aspect of this design is that it, like others, asks individuals to write about a time they felt a given emotion (here, anger) *about politics*. Because such a design pairs an emotional stimulus with a prompt that causes an individual to think *specifically* about politics or political events, it is difficult to disentangle whether anger is causing a shift in attitudes toward the national government or if merely thinking about politics alters individuals' evaluations of governmental performance. Therefore, as a robustness check on the traditional emotional recall design, I included two additional treatment groups into which respondents could have been randomized. One treatment group asked participants to "write about a time they were very angry." The other treatment group asked individuals to "write about a time they thought about politics." By separating the emotion (anger) from the target (politics) in this way, I am able to more precisely control the causal mechanism being manipulated. This also allows for a straightforward examination as to the role of targeted political anger and generalized apolitical anger in shaping citizens' views

---

[3] Such an approach is not the only way to alter individuals' emotional states. Lab experiments facilitate a wider range of experimental manipulations – such as games or human interactions – but are impractical within the context of a survey experiment. For an excellent overview of "how to push someone's buttons," see Lobbestael, Arntz, and Wiers (2008).

TABLE 4.1 *Experimental design*

		Anger	
		Yes	No
Politics	Yes	Targeted political anger	Political salience
	No	Generalized anger	Control

This table shows the 2 × 2 design used for the experiment in this chapter. Respondents were randomized into one of these four groups.

of the national government. A schematic of the experimental design is shown in Table 4.1.

To help facilitate an easier understanding of the experimental conditions, consider the following examples of responses to each of the treatment groups. One individual who was randomized into the anger about politics condition wrote that "the lack of action on social security pisses me off – it seems congress always waits till [sic] the very last minute to fix issues with it that need fixing." Another individual wrote that "[o]ur country is going to crap because politicians care more about themselves and their own personal agendas then [sic] they do the welfare of the country and its people." Individuals who were randomized into the apolitical anger condition wrote about their divorce, problems their children were having at school, and confrontations with former romantic partners. Those individuals who were randomized into the political salience condition tended to write about noteworthy political events, such as the assassination of Robert Kennedy.

Finally, after survey participants were randomized into one of the treatment groups described above, they were asked to rate their level of agreement with the following statement: "The national government is unresponsive to the concerns and interests of the public." Agreement with this statement was measured on a 0–10 scale, where 0 indicates that an individual "completely disagrees" with the statement and 10 indicates that an individual "completely agrees" with the statement.

Recall that the expectation is that higher levels of anger should cause individuals to view the national government as unresponsive to the concerns and interests of the public. Comparing the mean scores on this metric by treatment status provides suggestive evidence that such a relationship exists. The mean rating on this scale for individuals who were randomized into the "write about a time you were very angry" treatment condition is 7.0; the mean score for those randomized into the "write about a time you were very angry about politics" treatment condition

TABLE 4.2 *Effect of anger on trust in government*

	Govt. Unresponsiveness	
Anger	0.277**	0.256**
	(0.122)	(0.119)
Anger about politics	0.195*	0.204*
	(0.118)	(0.116)
Think about politics	0.182	0.193
	(0.120)	(0.117)
Controls	No	Yes
N	3,188	3,141
R^2	0.002	0.057

$*p < .1; **p < .05; ***p < .01.$
These experimental results show that inducing higher levels of anger causes
individuals to have lower levels of trust in the national government.
Specifically, priming individuals to become angrier makes them more likely
to believe that the national government is unresponsive to the concerns and
interests of the public.

is 6.91; the mean score for those who were randomized into the "write
about a time you thought about politics" treatment condition is a similar
6.90; finally, the mean score on this metric for those in the control group
is 6.72.

In order to more definitively test whether anger has a causal effect in
reducing trust in government, I regressed the measure of trust in government described above on indicators for treatment status. The expectation
is that the coefficients for the anger treatment conditions should be positively signed. The results of the experimental manipulations are shown in
Table 4.2.

The first column of Table 4.2 presents the experimental results without
any control variables included. Those who were randomized into both
the generalized apolitical anger ($p < .05$) and the anger-about-politics
($p < .1$) treatment groups were more likely to agree that the national
government is unresponsive to the concerns and interests of the public.
Merely thinking about politics had no effect on belief in government
responsiveness. The second column adds a series of control variables –
ideology, partisanship, level of education, income, and dummy variables
for non-Whites and females – to the original model specification.[4] With

---

[4] Adding a series of control variables to a model that is estimated on experimental data
accomplishes two things: first, given that the coefficients change very little between the
unconditional and the conditional models, we can have a high degree of confidence that the

these control variables included, the coefficients remain quite similar to those in the unconditional regression: those who were randomized into the anger condition and those were randomized into the anger-about-politics condition both exhibited a greater belief that the national government is unresponsive to the concerns and interests of the public. Thus, regardless of the exact wording of the experimental prime, heightened levels of anger causes individuals to have lower evaluations of American government.[5]

While both generalized and targeted political anger were able to lower Americans' trust in the national government, it is striking that the treatment effect for generalized anger is more reliably distinguishable from zero than is the treatment effect for targeted political anger. This suggests that anger in one area of a person's life can easily "spill over" and affect evaluations and interpretations of unrelated events – a finding in line with the psychological literature on emotions. Apolitical anger, then, can affect views of political objects.

In addition to the fact that generalized apolitical anger is able to lower respondents' evaluations of the national government, one particularly noteworthy result from the experimental manipulation is that the causal effect for those individuals who were randomized into the treatment group that asked them to write about a time they thought about politics is almost identical to the effect for those who were randomized into the treatment group that sought to prime anger specifically about politics. Given that anger – and not an increase in the salience of politics or political issues – is the theorized causal mechanism through which the reduction in trust in government occurs, the fact that these two causal effects are so similar is puzzling.

Therefore, in order to more precisely determine the ways in which the causal manipulations affected survey respondents, I conducted a sentiment analysis on the text written by individuals during the emotional recall design. To this end, I utilized the Linguistic Inquiry and Word Count (LIWC) dictionary as my classification system. Developed by psychologists and linguists, LIWC analyzes both the grammatical (e.g., number of pronouns or adverbs) and psychological structures (e.g.,

---

randomization process worked as intended; and, second, it helps alleviate any infelicities that might have occurred during randomization.
5 While different treatment wordings were both able to successfully induce anger in survey participants, there is no statistically significant difference between the "anger" coefficient and the "anger-about-politics" coefficient.

degree of negatively or positively valenced words) of a segment of text. Because "[l]anguage is the most common and reliable way for people to translate their internal thoughts and emotions into a form that others can understand," and because "words ...are the very stuff of psychology and communication" (Tausczik and Pennebaker 2010), understanding the types of words and phrases that individuals used in their emotional recall response will shed light on the specific emotions that they were experiencing during the experimental manipulation.[6]

Of particular interest is the degree to which individuals used words that are indicative of being angry or upset. Among others, such words include "anger," "rage," "hate," or "outrage." Of additional interest is the amount of "negative emotional" or "positive emotional" words. The former metric is an aggregate measure of negatively valenced emotional words, such as those dealing with anger, sadness, frustration, or anxiety; this is in contrast to the latter measure, which is an aggregation of positively valenced emotional words, such as happiness, joy, or anticipation.

If the experimental manipulations worked as intended, individuals who were randomized into the "write about a time you were very angry" and "write about a time you were angry about politics" conditions should use language that is indicative of expressions of anger. These individuals should also write responses that are higher in negative emotional words and lower in positive emotional words. Relative to the control group, individuals who were randomized into the "write about a time you thought about politics" condition should not be more likely to use words that indicate being in a heightened state of anger. They should also not be more likely to use negative emotional words.

To examine whether this is the case, I regressed a series of LIWC word classification variables on dummy variables for each treatment status. Specifically, I regressed the percentage of angry words, the percentage of negative emotional words, and the percentage of positive emotional words that an individual used in her emotional recall text on indicator variables for treatment group assignment. If the causal manipulations worked according to the theoretical expectations, then individuals who were randomized into the anger-only and the anger-about-politics treatment groups should have a comparatively higher percentage of angry and negative emotional words in their emotional recall text. Individuals in these two groups should also have comparatively fewer positive

---

[6] For more information on how words are indicative of personality and emotional states, see Allport and Odbert's (1936) discussion of the "lexical hypothesis."

emotional words in their text. Conversely, there is no firm theoretical reason to assume that individuals who were randomized into the "write about a time you thought about politics" treatment group should have either higher or lower percentages of angry, negative emotional, or positive emotional words in their emotional recall text.[7]

The results in Table 4.3 suggests that the experimental manipulation largely worked as intended. Relative to the control group, those individuals who were randomized into the treatment group that asked them to write about a time they were very angry wrote emotional recall responses with 3.4% more angry words, 4.5% more negative emotional words, and 3.4% fewer positive emotional words. Compared to the control group, individuals who were randomized into the treatment group that sought to prime anger specifically about politics wrote responses with 2.7% more angry words, 3.7% more negative emotional words, and 2.4% fewer positive emotional words. In all cases, the treatment condition that sought to prime anger about apolitical issues was the most effective in actually heightening individuals' level of anger. These findings help to explain why this treatment condition (contrary to theoretical expectations) appears to have had the strongest causal effect in reducing individuals' trust in government, as shown in Table 4.2.

Interestingly, the treatment group that asked individuals to write about a time they thought about politics also led to more angry and negatively valenced emotional recall responses. Indeed, individuals who were randomized into this treatment group used nearly 1% more angry words and 2% more negative emotional words than those in the control group. However, individuals in this treatment condition were not likely to use any fewer positive emotional words in their responses than those in the control group. This suggests that merely asking individuals to think about politics is sufficient to induce a degree of anger. It appears, then, as if politics and negative emotions are not entirely separable. That this finding exists also helps to explain why the effects of the "write about a time you were angry about politics" and "write about a time you thought about politics" treatment groups are nearly identical: both trigger heightened levels of individual anger.

---

7 Indeed, it is possible to imagine that individuals could either become inspired by thinking about politics (and so write from a positive emotional standpoint) or become upset or outraged by thinking about politics (and so write from a negative emotional standpoint).

TABLE 4.3 *Sentiment analysis by treatment status*

	Pct. Angry Words	Pct. Negative Emotions	Pct. Positive Emotions
Angry	3.410***	4.461***	−3.370***
	(0.191)	(0.304)	(0.789)
Angry about politics	2.672***	3.705***	−2.406***
	(0.186)	(0.296)	(0.768)
Think about politics	0.938***	1.962***	−1.119
	(0.188)	(0.300)	(0.778)
Constant	0.080	0.942***	7.604***
	(0.131)	(0.209)	(0.542)
N	3,088	3,088	3,088
R^2	0.116	0.078	0.007

*$p < .1$; **$p < .05$; ***$p < .01$.

This table confirms that the experimental design worked as intended. Indeed, those who were randomized into the apolitical anger and political anger treatment conditions used more angry words and more negative emotional words than those in the control group.

4.4 THE MAGNITUDE IS WHAT MATTERS

The results shown in column 1 of Table 4.3 indicate that the three treatment groups produced different mean levels of anger in survey respondents. These differences across the treatment groups allows for an examination of the relationship between the dosage of anger one received during the randomization process and the extent to which he or she expresses distrust in the government. In other words, the fact that the amount of anger survey respondents exhibited varied according to their treatment status that allows us to understand whether higher magnitudes of anger produced greater amounts of distrust in the government.

In order to examine the relationship between the magnitude, or dosage, of anger and distrust in government, I adopt an instrumental variables approach. Specifically, I use the three treatment assignments as an instrument for the percentage of angry words that individuals used in their responses after receiving their emotional recall prompt. The instrumented percentage of angry words, then, is used to predict the degree to which survey respondents expressed distrust in the national government. Such an approach is useful for two primary reasons. First, because the instruments are randomly assigned they are unrelated to individuals' ex ante levels of trust in the government. Second, the instruments are clearly related to the percentage of angry words survey respondents used in their stories, as shown in Table 4.3. Formally, the first stage regression is:

$$\text{Pct. Angry Words}_i = \alpha + \beta_1 \text{Anger}_i + \beta_2 \text{Political Anger}_i$$
$$+ \beta_3 \text{Political Salience}_i + \epsilon$$

which is identical to the regression displayed in Table 4.3, column 1. The second stage regression is:

$$\text{Distrust}_i = \alpha + \beta_1 \widehat{\text{Pct. Angry Words}}_i + \epsilon$$

where β_1 is the instrumented percentage of angry words that individual i used in their response to the emotional recall prompt. If higher dosages of anger produced a greater amount of distrust in government, we should expect to see the instrumented variable in the second stage regression have a positively signed coefficient. As the first stage regression is already shown in Table 4.3, column 1, only the results from the second stage of the instrumental variables regression are shown in Table 4.4.

As shown in Table 4.4, those individuals who were induced by the instrument into using a greater percentage of angry words in their stories expressed a greater amount of distrust in the government. This finding suggests that, rather than the specific *source* of the anger, what is most important in terms of reducing an individual's level of trust in the government is the *magnitude* of their anger. The validity of this finding is corroborated by the strength of the instrument. Indeed, the F-statistic

TABLE 4.4 *The magnitude is what matters*

	Govt. Unresponsive
Predicted % angry words	0.066**
	(0.033)
Constant	6.760***
	(0.074)
Observations	3,065
F-statistic (first stage)	134.442***

$*p < .1; **p < .05; ***p < .01.$
This table shows the results of the second stage of the instrumental variables regression described in Section 4.4. The results indicate that higher levels of anger lead to a great amount of distrust in the government.

from the first stage of the instrumental variables regression is 134. As instruments with a F-statistic greater than 10 are generally thought of as strong instruments, the F-statistic from this regression indicates that the variance in the predicted percentage of angry words that individuals used in their stories is largely driven by their assignment to one of the three treatment groups.[8]

4.5 EXTERNAL VALIDATION

Though the preceding analyses showed a causal effect of anger on trust in government, it is possible that the results are an artifact of the data being obtained during the 2016 presidential campaign. Moreover, while experiments are prized for their internal validity, they are oftentimes criticized for not providing results derived from "the real world." Therefore, as a way to check the temporal and external validity of the experimental results, I utilize data from the 2012 American National Election Studies (ANES) panel survey to examine the relationship between anger and trust in government in an additional national survey.

One drawback of using the ANES is that it does not contain a question that measures individuals' level of political anger or apolitical anger. Therefore, I rely on a series of proxy variables to analyze the relationship between anger and trust in government in the ANES data. Key for the analysis here are questions that asked about individuals' emotional feelings toward the Democratic and Republican presidential candidates, and a series of questions designed to measure individuals' level of trust in government. In order to construct the main independent variables of targeted political anger used in these analyses, I relied on individuals' responses to questions asking how often they felt angry at the Democratic presidential candidate and the Republican presidential candidate. These questions

---

[8] One potential concern about these results is whether or not the instrument satisfies the "exclusion restriction." In other words, one might wonder whether the instrument affects individuals' trust in government through some mechanism other than the elicitation of anger. While it is true that a residual amount of emotions other than anger were elicited by the random assignment to one of the three treatment conditions (as shown in Table 4.3, column 2), the strength of the instrument suggests that any bias that might arise due to a failure to meet the exclusion restriction is minimal. Indeed, because "the sensitivity of the [instrumental variables] estimator ...to violations of the exclusion restriction depends on the strength of the instruments" (Conley, Hansen, and Rossi 2008), there is little reason to worry about any bias in the estimates presented in Table 4.4 due to violations of the exclusion restriction.

have five possible responses, ranging from "never" to "always."[9] I used these variables to create a measure of anger toward the opposing party's presidential candidate, where Republican respondents' values are those reported on the measure tapping anger toward the Democratic presidential candidate, and Democratic respondents' values are those reported on the measure of anger toward the Republican presidential candidate. This measure of anger toward the opposing party's presidential candidate is scored such that higher values indicate more frequently feeling angry about the opposing party's presidential candidate.[10]

To measure generalized apolitical anger, I calculated the frequency with which respondents felt angry at *either* of the candidates from the two major parties. Though not a perfect operationalization of generalized anger, this measure has been previously used within the literature on emotions and politics (see, e.g., Valentino et al. 2011). As with the measure of targeted political anger, this measure is coded such that higher values indicate higher levels of anger.

There are three dependent variables in this analysis, each of which taps a different measure of citizens' trust in government. The first question asks individuals how many people in government they believe to be crooked. There are three possible responses to this question: "hardly any," "not very many," and "quite a few." The variable is coded to range from 1 to 3. The second question asks respondents to indicate whether they agree with the notion that public officials do not care what people think. Potential responses for this question range from "disagree strongly" to "agree strongly." The last dependent variable measures how much individuals believe that they have no say in what government does. Responses to this question range from "not at all" to "a great deal." For both of these variables, potential responses are coded to range from 1 to 5. In each case, higher values on these variables indicate lower levels of trust in government.

---

[9] The full range of possible responses are "never," "some of the time," "about half the time," "most of the time," and "always."

[10] It is important to note that the questions used to create these measures are the second part of a branching item in the 2012 ANES. The first question in the two-item series asks individuals whether they ever reported feeling angry at the Democratic or Republican presidential candidate. Only those individuals who answered "yes" are branched into this second question that reports the frequency of anger. As a robustness check, I also analyzed the models with the first question of the branch as the key independent variable. This question simply asks whether the respondent ever reported feeling angry at the Democratic (or Republican) presidential candidate. The results are robust to this change.

In order to minimize any confounding effects in my model estimates, I include in each model controls for partisanship, self-reported ideology (along a 7-point scale), gender, race, education, and a scale measuring an individual's level of activism. The education control is a trichotomous measure (1 = HS education or less; 2 = BA degree; 3 = graduate or professional degree), while the activism scale measures how many of eleven different participatory acts an individual engaged in. These acts are attending a rally, talking to others about politics, displaying a yard sign or a bumper sticker, working for a political party, donating money to a candidate, donating money to a party, donating to a third-party political organization, attending a march or rally, attending a school board meeting, signing a political petition, or contacting a Member of Congress about an issue. Additionally, in order to address concerns about answers to the post-election-dependent variables measuring trust in government being affected by the outcome of the election, I also include a pre-election measure of how much individuals trust the government as a control variable in each model. This allows for a de facto "baseline" level of trust in government to be built into the model estimates.

Finally, because much of the literature suggests that the strength of an individual's partisanship plays an outsized role in predicting political behavior (see, e.g., Abramowitz 2010; Bafumi and Shapiro 2009), I also include a dummy variable indicating whether an individual identifies as a "strong" partisan. Thus, this variable takes on a value of one for an individual who identifies as a "strong Democrat" or a "strong Republican" and a value of zero for those who do not.

To facilitate an easier interpretation of the relationship between the independent variables and the various metrics tapping into trust in government, all of the independent variables are normalized to range from 0 to 1. Estimation is via ordinary-least squares (OLS) regression. However, because each of the dependent variables has just a few possible categorical responses, I also estimated these models via a series of ordered logistic regressions. In each case, the findings are robust to the use of an ordered logit. Accordingly, I present OLS results here for ease of interpretation. Results of the models calculated using ordered logit are available in Table 4.6 in the Appendix. Additional model specifications can be found in the Appendix, Tables 4.7–4.10.

Across each of the three measures of trust in government, the results of Table 4.5 suggest that higher levels of targeted political anger and generalized apolitical anger are associated with a lower level of trust in government. The predictive power of anger toward the opposing

TABLE 4.5 *Anger and trust in government, external validity*

	Govt. Crooked		Govt. Cares		Have Say in Govt.	
Anger	0.166***	0.361**	0.553***	1.478***	0.492***	1.429***
	(0.053)	(0.170)	(0.116)	(0.367)	(0.133)	(0.419)
Democrat	−0.120***	−0.030	−0.288***	−0.278**	−0.386***	−0.235*
	(0.031)	(0.057)	(0.064)	(0.123)	(0.074)	(0.140)
Ideology	0.083	−0.004	−0.272	−0.356	−0.608***	−0.354
	(0.079)	(0.136)	(0.179)	(0.301)	(0.205)	(0.344)
Female	0.059**	0.035	0.031	0.222*	0.085	0.311**
	(0.028)	(0.054)	(0.059)	(0.119)	(0.068)	(0.136)
Non-White	0.099***	−0.016	0.108	0.067	−0.053	−0.003
	(0.032)	(0.057)	(0.070)	(0.125)	(0.080)	(0.142)
Education	−0.233***	−0.269***	−0.292***	−0.095	−0.374***	−0.100
	(0.044)	(0.084)	(0.090)	(0.179)	(0.104)	(0.204)
Activism	−0.044	−0.006	−0.397**	−0.235	−0.922***	−1.073***
	(0.074)	(0.137)	(0.154)	(0.290)	(0.177)	(0.331)
Pre-election trust	−0.653***	−0.149	−1.237***	−0.877*	−0.959***	−1.061*
	(0.092)	(0.201)	(0.216)	(0.489)	(0.247)	(0.558)
Strong partisan	−0.087***	−0.157**	−0.154**	−0.347**	−0.147**	−0.427***
	(0.029)	(0.063)	(0.063)	(0.142)	(0.072)	(0.162)
Constant	2.875***	2.745***	4.487***	4.002***	4.382***	3.663***
	(0.075)	(0.144)	(0.171)	(0.332)	(0.196)	(0.379)
Anger type	Targeted	Generalized	Targeted	Generalized	Targeted	Generalized
N	1,577	429	1,162	324	1,162	324
R^2	0.078	0.058	0.096	0.122	0.116	0.149

* $p < .1$; ** $p < .05$; *** $p < .01$.

This table shows that the relationship between anger and trust in government can be replicated in an observational dataset. The relationship between anger and lower levels of trust in government is robust to the use of two different measures of anger. Note that all independent variables are scaled to range from 0 to 1.

party's presidential candidate is quite impressive. Indeed, in all six model specifications, the coefficient estimate of anger toward the opposing party's presidential candidate is larger, in terms of absolute value, than the dummy variables for gender and race. The coefficient estimate for the anger variable is larger than that of the activism variable in all but one of the model specifications and is consistently on par with an individual's level of education in terms of its predictive ability.

Because the majority of the literature on trust in government focuses on the role of partisanship, comparing the standardized coefficient estimates between the anger variable and the partisan dummy is particularly important. A simple comparison shows that anger is an important predictor of how much an individual trust the national government. Indeed, the coefficient for anger is larger than both the Democratic dummy variable and the strong partisan dummy variable in all six model specifications. This suggests that, while partisanship continues to powerfully shape the ways in which Americans view the political world, having higher levels of anger also plays a substantively important role in altering levels of trust in government.

One question about these results is whether or not they are robust to the inclusion of a control variable measuring an individual's amount of targeted anxiety or generalized anxiety. When the models presented in Table 4.5 are re-estimated with measures of anxiety included (calculated in the same manner as the anger measures), anger remains statistically significant in only two of the models. Similarly, anxiety is statistically significant in only two of the models. These models are presented in Table 4.11 in the Appendix to this chapter.

However, rather than casting doubt on the external validity of the results presented above, the fact that anger loses its predictive power in these models is likely due to the multicollinearity produced by including both anger and anxiety in the same model specification. Indeed, the generalized measures of anger and anxiety correlate at .74 and the targeted measures of anger and anxiety correlate at .62. Such high correlations are almost certainly driven by the fact that these emotions are both negatively valenced and are elicited by common sources (either Barack Obama or Mitt Romney). Such a high degree of multicollinearity in these observational data serves to further highlight the importance of the experiment in Section 4.3, which disentangled the effects of anger and anxiety on trust in government and showed a clear and robust causal effect of anger on declining trust in government.

4.6 CONCLUSION AND DISCUSSION

Partisanship in the American electorate has changed in dramatic ways over the past few decades. While Americans used to feel indifferent toward the opposing political party, the contemporary era is defined by intense dislike of the out-party, its supporters, and its preferred policies. This new partisan orientation has caused Americans to be more biased against the opposing party (Mason 2015; Sood and Iyengar 2015), and, along with the decline of the incumbency advantage in favor of partisan identification (Jacobson 2015), to vote increasingly straight-ticket (Abramowitz and Webster 2016).

Yet, outside of these behavioral outcomes, little has been done to understand how and why this anger-fueled negative partisan affect shapes Americans' views of the national government. In this chapter, I have helped to fill this gap by showing how anger – both political and apolitical – is associated with lower levels of trust in government. Specifically, higher levels of anger are associated with the belief that people in government are crooked, that public officials do not care what people think, and that citizens have no say in what the government does. I have also shown through a survey experiment on a national sample of registered voters that political anger has a causal effect in reducing citizens' trust in government. This diminution in trust in the national government is due to the fact that people tend to evaluate objects in ways that are in line with their emotions: because anger is an emotion with a negative valence, and because this anger is directed at the government and those who run it, individuals who are angry have poor evaluations of the national government.

Importantly, the experimental results I have shown here indicate that generalized apolitical anger can also lower Americans' trust in the national government. This suggests that the negative valence associated with apolitical anger can spill over to political targets. From the standpoint of campaign strategy, this implies that the ways in which members of the electorate view politics and political affairs can be shaped in subtle ways. Indeed, rather than seeking to stir anger specifically about the government or opposition candidates within the electorate, political parties and candidates merely need to incite generic anger in order to alter patterns of public opinion. That anger of an apolitical nature can affect evaluations of the national government suggests that the *magnitude*, and not the *source*, is the most important factor in anger's ability to shape patterns of public opinion.

Moreover, these findings do not appear to be limited to one specific period of time. The data for the experimental analysis presented in Section 4.3 was collected in October 2016. The correlational analyses presented in Section 4.5 utilized the 2012 ANES panel data. Thus, the experimental results were obtained nearly four years after the final wave of the 2012 ANES panel was completed. That these findings are produced in two different datasets, fielded almost four years apart from each other, suggests that anger has a robust role in altering citizens' level of trust in the national government.

Finally, the results of my analyses suggest that politics and anger are closely intertwined. A sentiment analysis on the text of the emotional recall responses derived from the experimental manipulation indicates that merely asking individuals to think about politics prompts them to exhibit higher levels of anger and other negatively valenced emotions. Accordingly, it appears as though politics and anger are, to a certain extent, inseparable.

Normatively, the results presented here have troubling implications. With the rise of negative partisan affect and a contentious style of governing, Americans are more frequently exposed to anger-inducing stimuli. With politics increasingly being defined by feelings of anger toward the opposing party and its governing elite, trust in government is bound to decline. Absent some exogenous shock to the political system that reverses this trend, it is possible that trust in government will decline to a level so low that the national government will lose its sense of legitimacy in the eyes of those to whom it is accountable. If trust in governing institutions reaches such a level, the health of American democracy is threatened.

Future research, then, should examine how the harmful effects of anger in modern-day politics can be mitigated. Relatedly, future work should examine how long the effects of anger on reducing trust in government persist. Is anger an emotion that brings negative evaluations of governmental institutions, but only temporarily? Or, do the effects of anger on reducing citizens' trust in government last long after anger has subsided? Understanding the duration of these effects will help to clarify our understanding about the linkage between the hostile nature of contemporary politics and Americans' trust in their own government. With trust in government continuing to decline (Pew Research Center 2015; The Economist 2017), understanding these processes is essential to strengthening American democracy.

4.7 APPENDIX

TABLE 4.6 *Regression estimates of trust in government (ordered logit)*

	Govt. Crooked	Govt. Cares	Have Say in Govt.
Anger	0.605***	1.040***	0.761***
	(0.209)	(0.217)	(0.214)
N	1,577	1,162	1,162

*p < .1; **p < .05; ***p < .01.

This table shows that the results derived from models estimated via OLS are robust to using a series of ordered logits. Models are calculated with the same control variables used in the primary estimation. Note that all independent variables are scaled to range from 0 to 1.

TABLE 4.7 *Regression estimates of trust in government, additional dependent variables*

	Govt. Does What Is Right OLS	Govt. Wastes Money OLS	Govt. Run by Big Interests Logit
Anger	0.347***	0.051	0.208
	(0.077)	(0.033)	(0.185)
Democrat	−0.374***	−0.302***	−0.486***
	(0.045)	(0.019)	(0.113)
Ideology	−0.135	−0.021	0.197
	(0.108)	(0.047)	(0.260)
Female	−0.078*	−0.032*	−0.404***
	(0.041)	(0.018)	(0.101)
Non-White	−0.126***	−0.051**	−0.490***
	(0.047)	(0.020)	(0.108)
Education	0.047	−0.148***	−0.033
	(0.064)	(0.027)	(0.156)
Activism	−0.212*	0.029	0.374
	(0.110)	(0.047)	(0.271)
Pre-election trust	3.806***	2.938***	2.019***
	(0.092)	(0.040)	(0.227)
N	1,529	3,114	3,083
R^2	0.082	0.109	

*p < .1; **p < .05; ***p < .01.

This table shows the relationship between targeted political anger and trust in government across three additional metrics. Note that all independent variables are scaled to range from 0 to 1.

TABLE 4.8 *Regression estimates of trust in government, accounting for strength of partisanship (standardized)*

	Govt. Crooked	Govt. Cares	Have Say in Govt.
Anger	0.045***	0.151***	0.134***
	(0.014)	(0.032)	(0.036)
Democrat	−0.060***	−0.144***	−0.193***
	(0.015)	(0.032)	(0.037)
Ideology	0.017	−0.056	−0.125***
	(0.016)	(0.037)	(0.042)
Female	0.029**	0.015	0.043
	(0.014)	(0.029)	(0.034)
Non-White	0.049***	0.053	−0.026
	(0.016)	(0.034)	(0.039)
Education	−0.077***	−0.096***	−0.123***
	(0.014)	(0.030)	(0.034)
Activism	−0.008	−0.072**	−0.167***
	(0.013)	(0.028)	(0.032)
Pre-election trust	−0.116***	−0.220***	−0.171***
	(0.016)	(0.038)	(0.044)
Strong partisan	−0.042***	−0.075**	−0.071**
	(0.014)	(0.031)	(0.035)
Constant	2.631***	3.802***	3.367***
	(0.015)	(0.033)	(0.037)
N	1,577	1,162	1,162
R^2	0.078	0.096	0.116

*$p < .1$; **$p < .05$; ***$p < .01$.

This table shows the standardized coefficients across each of the three model specifications. In each case, the coefficient on the anger variable is bigger – in terms of absolute value – than the coefficient on the dummy variable for strong partisans.

TABLE 4.9 *Regression estimates of trust in government among democrats*

	Govt. Crooked	Govt. Cares	Have Say in Govt.
Anger	0.052	0.371**	0.198
	(0.074)	(0.164)	(0.184)
Ideology	−0.007	−0.300	−0.532*
	(0.106)	(0.247)	(0.277)
Female	0.038	0.008	0.103
	(0.041)	(0.087)	(0.097)
Non-White	0.126***	0.081	0.039
	(0.042)	(0.090)	(0.101)
Education	−0.222***	−0.258*	−0.360**
	(0.064)	(0.135)	(0.151)
Activism	−0.188*	−0.808***	−1.305***
	(0.101)	(0.212)	(0.237)
Pre-election trust	−0.525***	−1.273***	−1.107***
	(0.120)	(0.276)	(0.309)

(*Continued*)

	Govt. Crooked	Govt. Cares	Have Say in Govt.
Strong partisan	2.801***	4.357***	4.132***
	(0.099)	(0.220)	(0.246)
N	844	590	590
R^2	0.054	0.081	0.113

*$p < .1$; **$p < .05$; ***$p < .01$.

This shows the relationship between anger and trust in government for those respondents who self-identify as Democrats. Though the relationship between anger and trust in government is weaker here than in the original specification found in the chapter (Table 4.5), the results still suggest that anger shapes the ways in which citizens view the national government. Note that all independent variables are scaled to range from 0 to 1.

TABLE 4.10 *Regression estimates of trust in government, with generalized measures of anger and alternative dependent variables*

	Govt. Does What Is Right OLS	Govt. Wastes Money OLS	Govt. Run by Big Interests Logit
Anger	0.925***	0.130	2.082***
	(0.253)	(0.111)	(0.745)
Democrat	−0.140*	−0.200***	−0.269
	(0.083)	(0.037)	(0.234)
Ideology	−0.131	−0.133	−0.995*
	(0.210)	(0.091)	(0.581)
Female	−0.114	−0.019	−0.297
	(0.078)	(0.035)	(0.214)
Non-White	−0.174**	−0.004	−0.382*
	(0.086)	(0.037)	(0.222)
Education	−0.161	−0.186***	−0.445
	(0.116)	(0.053)	(0.322)
Activism	−0.328	0.031	0.702
	(0.211)	(0.091)	(0.579)
Strong partisan	−0.100	−0.029	−0.578**
	(0.091)	(0.040)	(0.234)
Constant	3.741***	2.938***	2.445***
	(0.178)	(0.078)	(0.498)
N	419	849	843
R^2	0.077	0.065	
Adjusted R^2	0.059	0.056	
Log likelihood			−309.898
Residual Std. Error	0.784 (df = 410)	0.498 (df = 840)	
F-statistic	4.276*** (df = 8; 410)	7.290*** (df = 8; 840)	
AIC			637.796

*$p < .1$; **$p < .05$; ***$p < .01$.

This table shows that generalized apolitical anger is still predictive of trust in government across different dependent variables, and while controlling for strength of partisanship. Note that all independent variables are scaled to range from 0 to 1.

TABLE 4.11 *Anger and trust in government external validity check, with anxiety*

	Govt. Crooked		Govt. Cares		Have Say in Govt.	
Anger	0.101	−0.106	0.435***	−0.731	0.322*	−0.029
	(0.077)	(0.402)	(0.167)	(0.769)	(0.192)	(1.034)
Anxiety	0.089	0.119	0.253*	1.622**	0.103	0.721
	(0.071)	(0.366)	(0.153)	(0.730)	(0.176)	(0.981)
Democrat	−0.143***	−0.096	−0.331***	−0.464**	−0.488***	−0.240
	(0.035)	(0.105)	(0.073)	(0.216)	(0.084)	(0.291)
Ideology	0.106	−0.049	−0.265	−0.676	−0.590**	−0.429
	(0.092)	(0.237)	(0.204)	(0.470)	(0.235)	(0.632)
Female	0.075**	0.058	−0.028	0.231	0.024	0.583**
	(0.031)	(0.104)	(0.066)	(0.211)	(0.076)	(0.283)
Non-White	0.063*	−0.035	0.083	0.121	0.033	0.047
	(0.038)	(0.105)	(0.082)	(0.207)	(0.094)	(0.279)
Education	−0.217***	−0.179	−0.205**	−0.029	−0.379***	0.241
	(0.048)	(0.158)	(0.099)	(0.313)	(0.114)	(0.421)
Activism	−0.094	0.482*	−0.563***	0.132	−0.851***	−0.820
	(0.080)	(0.253)	(0.167)	(0.506)	(0.192)	(0.680)
Pre-election trust	−0.637***	−0.378	−1.310***	−3.898***	−0.766**	−2.516*
	(0.107)	(0.420)	(0.248)	(1.048)	(0.285)	(1.409)
Strong partisan	−0.095***	0.043	−0.183***	−0.492*	−0.155*	−0.296
	(0.033)	(0.126)	(0.070)	(0.254)	(0.081)	(0.341)
Constant	2.871***	2.882***	4.508***	5.568***	4.416***	4.250***
	(0.090)	(0.289)	(0.199)	(0.605)	(0.229)	(0.813)
Anger and anxiety type	Targeted	Generalized	Targeted	Generalized	Targeted	Generalized
N	1,149	108	895	86	895	86
R^2	0.093	0.077	0.116	0.405	0.119	0.176

*$p < .1$; **$p < .05$; ***$p < .01$.
This table replicates the models found in Table 4.5 but includes a control for anxiety. Note that all independent variables are scaled to range from 0 to 1.

5

Anger and Democratic Values in the Mass Public

Anger is one letter short of danger.
— Eleanor Roosevelt

Perhaps the most defining hallmark of the American political system is its enduring commitment to democracy and democratic values. Writing nearly 200 years ago in his now-famous *Democracy in America*, Alexis de Tocqueville (1835) argued that, despite the multitude of institutions and the complexity of American political society, there was a "sovereign power [that] exists above these institutions ...and these features which may destroy or modify them at its pleasure." This "sovereign power" to which Tocqueville was referring was the populace, whom he observed was able to exercise "a perpetual influence on society" by electing faithful public servants and removing those who acted outside of the public's interest. As such, Tocqueville's (1835) summation of political affairs in America was in line with a Jeffersonian view of democracy in which those who govern do so only for as long as the people allow.

Politicians throughout American history have pointed to the importance of maintaining and strengthening democracy and the democratic values that Tocqueville had observed. Franklin Delano Roosevelt, for instance, used an address in 1938 to remind his audience that "[t]he ultimate rulers of our democracy are not a President and Senators and Congressmen and Government officials but the voters of this country."[1] Ronald Reagan would later use a speech at a commemoration honoring

[1] FDR's speech, "Address at Marietta, Ohio," can read in full at www.presidency.ucsb.edu/ws/?pid=15672.

the fortieth anniversary of D-Day to tell those listening that protecting democracy was so important that it was worth dying for. According to Reagan, this was because democracy is "the most deeply honorable form of government ever devised by man."[2]

Yet, while American history is replete with politicians extolling the virtues of democracy and democratic values, the contemporary political landscape is one in which American citizens appear to be anything but fully committed to democracy being what Linz and Stepan (1996) refer to as "the only game in town." Indeed, a recent Pew Research Center report found that only 58% of Americans believe democracy is working "very" or "somewhat" well in the United States. This same report found that 61% of Americans believe that "significant" changes are necessary to the "fundamental design and structure of government." Moreover, in a break from democratic norms, the report indicates that Americans on both sides of the political divide are increasingly viewing the opposing party and its supporters as dangerous and hostile to the country's well-being.[3]

Why are Americans growing weary of democracy and expressing a weaker commitment to democratic norms and values? In this chapter, I argue that voters' heightened levels of anger toward the opposing political party is one of the primary reasons for Americans' weakening commitment to the norms and values that have long governed democratic competition. Moreover, I argue that these two phenomena are not simply correlated with each other but, instead, that anger actually causes citizens to express a lower commitment to democratic norms and values. This result is most pronounced in the area of political tolerance. Indeed, the results of the analyses in this chapter show that anger causes Americans to believe that supporters of the opposing political party are a threat to the country's well-being, and that those who disagree with them politically are less intelligent than they are. However, a follow-up study reveals that, while anger lowers citizens' commitment to democratic norms and values, it does not cause Americans to want to replace democracy with some other form of government. As a whole, the results indicate that anger in American politics has contributed to the decline in citizens' commitment

---

[2] Reagan's remarks can be found in full at www.washingtonpost.com/news/the-fix/wp/2014/06/05/watch-ronald-reagans-address-commemorating-the-40th-anniversary-of-d-day/?utm_term=.0803e4eff94b.

[3] The full report can be accessed at www.people-press.org/2018/04/26/the-public-the-political-system-and-american-democracy/.

to democratic norms and values. However, to the extent Americans are weakening in their commitment to the institutional structures of democracy itself, the cause appears to lie elsewhere.

To begin, I briefly sketch the voluminous literature on democracy and democratic norms.[4] I then discuss how anger has the ability to push citizens away from their commitment to these democratic norms. Next, I explicate a pair of research designs that exogenously vary individuals' level of anger before assessing attitudes about democracy. Finally, I present a series of results consistent with the idea that anger lowers citizens' commitment to democratic norms and values before concluding with a discussion about the implication of these findings for the future health of the American political system.

5.1 CONCEPTUALIZING DEMOCRACY

Indicative of its societal importance, no topic within political science has been studied more than democracy. From examining the origins of democracy (see, e.g., Acemoglu and Robinson 2006), to the processes of democratic transitions and consolidations (see, e.g., Bratton and van de Walle 1997; Linz and Stepan 1996), to the specific types of democracies (see, e.g., Lijphart 1999), to the functioning of democratic government in societies divided along various cleavages (see, e.g., Lijphart 1977; Norris 2008), political scientists have long been interested in understanding the nature of democracy and democratic government. The multitude of ways in which democracy has been studied means that scholars have been unable to agree on a precise way to define democracy. Yet, despite the lack of scholarly consensus, there are key indicators of democracy that are found in most definitions.

Writing over half a century ago, Lipset (1963) argued that a democratic society had two key aspects: "regular constitutional opportunities for changing ...governing officials" and a sufficiently large electorate such that the most people possible were able to choose their governing officials. Such a definition is similar to Lijphart's (1999), who relies on Abraham Lincoln's famous summation of democracy as "government by the people and for the people" as his operationalization of democracy. Moreover, these definitions find common ground with Bollen (1980), who argued

---

[4] As the scholarly literature on democracy is quite large, what follows will necessarily be an abridged and incomplete treatment of the subject.

that democracy is best defined as a political system in which "the political power of the elite is minimized and that of the nonelite is maximized."

Government is, as Lincoln said, "by the people and for the people," when certain criteria are met. Building on Lipset's (1963) notion that elections must be held at regular intervals, Przeworski (1991) adds two more criteria that must be met in order for a state to be called democratic. The first is that the outcome of any given election must not be known before the election occurs. Such a requirement distinguishes democracies from dictatorships, which may nominally hold elections but fix the result before any voting actually occurs. The second requirement that Przeworski (1991) identifies is that election results must be binding. Thus, in a democratic state, losers accept the outcome of the election as legitimate.

These definitions are succinctly captured by Dahl (1971). While arguing that no country meets the requirements necessary to be considered fully democratic, the closest ideal type to democratic perfection – what Dahl (1971) termed a "polyarchy" – can be thought to be comprised of two primary dimensions: contestation and inclusiveness. Contestation, according to Dahl (1971), refers to the extent to which citizens are able to articulate their preferences and have their wishes be considered by the government. Inclusiveness deals with who gets to participate in the political process and whether citizens' participation is weighted equally.

The above definitions are largely focused on the *process* of democracy. That is, they are focused on the "rules of the game" that dictate how politics and governing should be conducted (e.g., a constitutional order, universal or near-universal suffrage). Accordingly, I refer to these types of definitions as *functional definitions*. While these definitions are foundational to nearly all operationalizations of democracy, other scholars argue that states should possess more than just these functional characteristics. To be truly democratic, some argue, a state should have protections for individuals' civil rights and ensure a wide range of political liberties. States that have these characteristics are often referred to as *liberal democracies*.

Though questions about how many and what specific types of civil rights and political liberties must exist in order for a state to be deemed a liberal democracy, the literature overwhelmingly suggests that liberal democracies focus primarily on ensuring (to the greatest extent possible) a protection for minority rights and tolerance for those with opposing political views. Such tolerance can come through the form of freedom of expression in the media (Bollen 1993), the freedom to join political parties and social groups (Bollen and Paxton 2000), or some other guarantor of individual and group-based expression.

Though the above definitions are certainly far from exhaustive, they offer a useful guide as to how democracy and democratic norms should best be operationalized. For these purposes, I draw on functional definitions of democracy as well as indicators of liberal democracies in order to build multiple measures of commitment to democratic norms and values. In this chapter, I focus on three measures of democratic norms and values: (1) a commitment to a codified order that regulates the nature of governing and political competition; (2) tolerance for supporters of the opposing political party; and, finally, (3) respect for minority rights. Though examining only a few indicators of democracy necessarily leaves important elements out of the equation, focusing on these three aspects offers the benefit of empirical parsimony while still capturing perhaps the most important democratic norms and values.

5.2 ANGER AND DEMOCRATIC COMMITMENT

Thus far I have argued that a commitment to some standard or law regulating the process of governing and political competition, a tolerance for one's political opponents, and a respect for minority rights are three of the most important democratic norms and values. How, then, might heightened levels of anger toward the opposing political party and its supporters cause individuals to weaken in their commitment to these foundational principles?

To understand how anger can lead to lower levels of commitment to these democratic norms, it is important to understand the psychological underpinnings of emotions. Though emotions are often fleeting and can be aroused – perhaps unknowingly – by various stimuli, the precise ways in which they affect people are predictable. Such predictions draw on insights from the theory of Affective Intelligence, which argues that people only pay attention to politics when their emotions prompt them to do so (Marcus, Neuman, and MacKuen 2000).

Emotions, particularly those that are negatively valenced, tend to have one of two effects on individuals.[5] One response to a negatively valenced

---

5 "Negatively valenced" emotions include emotions such as anger, anxiety, fear, disgust, and sadness. This contrasts with "positively valenced" emotions such as happiness, joy, or contentment.

emotion is to seek out new information. Such a response is typical of those who are experiencing anxiety. For example, in their analysis of the role of anxiety in political behavior and public opinion, Albertson and Gadarian (2015) show that those individuals who are anxious – whether from threats of terrorism, immigration, or the outbreak of a disease – are likely to question their beliefs. As a result, these individuals tend to seek out new information and thereby learn about the political world.

While some negatively valenced emotions – such as anxiety – tend to make people seek out new information, others prompt individuals to "mentally retreat." That is, rather than seeking out new information, individuals experiencing certain negatively valenced emotions are likely to increase their reliance on the things they already know and believe. This act of "doubling down" on the beliefs, opinions, and knowledge that one already possesses is an act commonly engaged in by those who are in a heightened state of anger. Bodenhausen, Sheppard, and Kramer (1994) cogently illustrate anger's ability to push individuals toward an increased reliance on their beliefs and opinions by showing that heightened levels of anger cause people to draw upon racial and social stereotypes when making judgments.

In addition to increasing one's reliance on stereotypes and heuristics, anger has been found to increase the likelihood of conflict. Studying the relationship between dyads of business partners, Allred et al. (1997) show that business partners who have high levels of anger and low levels of compassion toward each other are more inclined to assign negative meanings to the other's actions. These negative meanings engender anger which, in turn, increases conflict and reduces the likelihood of future cooperation.

Such a finding is supported by a large body of literature that argues that, when individuals blame some other person or entity for an experienced wrongdoing, they direct their anger specifically toward that person or entity (see, e.g., Allred 1999; Bower 1991). Averill (1982) demonstrates that this directed anger is commonplace, showing that "the typical episode of anger involves an attribution of responsibility, an accusation, so to speak, that the target has done something wrong." Averill further notes that "normative" cases of anger (i.e., those instances in which anger is not directed at an inanimate or fictitious object) typically involve blame being directed toward a specific person, group of people, or institution.

This theoretical approach pairs with another, appraisal theory, which suggests that the extent to which an individual targets their anger toward another individual or entity is proportional to the degree to which they blame the other individual or entity for arousing the anger in the first place. Thus, the *"evaluations* and *interpretations* of events, rather than events per se," determine whether anger is experienced and to whom the emotional outburst is directed (Roseman, Spindel, and Jose 1990, emphasis mine).

In addition to being frequently directed at a specific person, group of people, or institution that is perceived to have caused an individual to become angry, anger is an emotion that typically causes some kind of reaction – whether physical, verbal, or something else entirely (Weiner 2000). Anger can lead to a multitude of reactions – for example, physical violence, verbal attacks, plotting ways to get even, and a heightened focus on the anger-inducing event. Oftentimes, multiple reactions occur when an individual is experiencing a heightened amount of anger (Averill 1982). The key takeaway is that emotional outbursts of anger lead to some sort of reaction or retaliation against that which elicited the anger (Lazarus and Smith 1988).

How might anger and appraisal theory apply to American politics? Moreover, how might the anger that is so prevalent within American politics cause citizens to weaken in their commitment to democratic norms and values? The literature described above suggests that emotional outbursts of anger require individuals to offer an attribution or blame for their anger and, accordingly, direct some sort of response or retaliation toward the offender. The current era of American politics is one in which anger and negativity are seemingly omnipresent (Abramowitz and Webster 2016, 2018*b*). Accordingly, the rancor and pervasiveness of partisan antipathy (Iyengar, Sood, and Lelkes 2012; Rogowski and Sutherland 2015; Webster and Abramowitz 2017) that defines the contemporary political era offers citizens plenty of opportunities to be made angry, to attribute blame to someone or some group for eliciting said anger, and for taking actions against those whom they blame.

A 2016 report from the Pew Research Center found that this anger and blame attribution is quite high. The Pew report notes that 46% of Republicans are made angry by the Democratic Party, while 47% of Democrats are similarly made angry by the Republican Party. This partisan anger is noteworthy because it has spilled over to assessments about the ways in which the opposing political party is harmful to the well-being of the country. Indeed, the Pew report found that 45% of Republicans believe that Democrats are a "threat to the nation's well-being." Among Democrats, 41% believe that Republicans pose a threat to the overall health of the country. Moreover, this anger appears to be quite personal: 27% of Republicans agreed that it would be hard to get along with a new neighbor if they were a Democrat, while 31% of Democrats claimed that it would be hard for them to get along with a new neighbor if he or she were a Republican. Such anger and dislike is likely reinforced by and, in turn, serves to reinforce, partisans' views of the opposing party's supporters as "closed-minded," "unintelligent," "immoral," and "dishonest."[6]

In addition to being angry specifically at the opposing party and its supporters, Americans today are frequently exposed to cues from political elites seeking to reinforce this anger and partisan affective polarization. In fact, one study found that elite incivility not only serves to elicit anger among the general public but also prompts individuals to engage in uncivil discourse themselves (Gervais 2016). A related study found that elite ideological polarization is associated with higher levels of affective polarization in the electorate (Banda and Cluverius 2018). With elite polarization continuing to rise, Americans are likely to be exposed to even more cues seeking to elicit anger toward the opposing political party and its supporters, a topic that was covered in detail in Chapter 2.

Rising anger, combined with political elites' deliberate perpetuation of anger among the electorate, means that Democrats and Republicans hold a tremendous amount of animosity toward each other. I argue that this anger and animosity has the effect of causing partisans to develop a desire to see their party "win" at all costs in fights with the opposing party – whether these fights are at the ballot box or in the halls of Congress. This desire to see one's side win at all costs will come at the expense of citizens' commitment to democratic norms and values that regulate governing and political competition. Put another way, anger should cause partisans to prioritize "victory" over the other side above winning "fairly" – that is, playing by the democratic "rules of the game." Thus, citizens weaken in their commitment to democratic norms and values when they are made angry at the opposing political party and desire partisan "victories" above all else. The causal pathway from anger to weakened democratic commitment is shown in Figure 5.1.

---

[6] The full Pew report, "Partisanship and Political Animosity in 2016," can be found here: www.people-press.org/2016/06/22/partisanship-and-political-animosity-in-2016/.

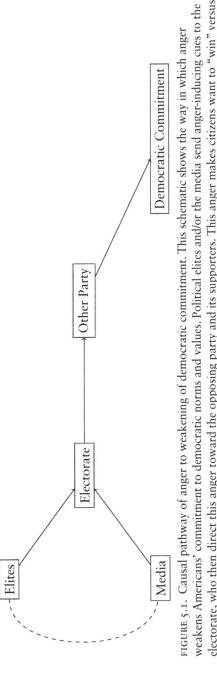

FIGURE 5.1. Causal pathway of anger to weakening of democratic commitment. This schematic shows the way in which anger weakens Americans' commitment to democratic norms and values. Political elites and/or the media send anger-inducing cues to the electorate, who then direct this anger toward the opposing party and its supporters. This anger makes citizens want to "win" versus the other party at all costs, which lessens their commitment to democratic norms and values.

5.3 EMPIRICAL EXAMINATION

5.3.1 Study Design

To examine the ways in which anger affects citizens' commitment to democratic norms and values, I employ a survey experiment that randomly induces anger in survey participants. The survey was fielded via the Lucid Fulcrum academic platform in January 2019. Though samples derived from Lucid are not nationally representative, they tend to perform better than most convenience samples (see, for instance, Coppock and McClellan 2018, on comparisons between Lucid, Amazon Mechanical Turk, and the American National Election Studies). In addition to the experimental manipulation, the survey contains a pre- and post-experiment survey. The pre-experiment survey measures individuals' partisan and ideological affiliation, both of which are measured on the typical 7-point scale that ranges from "strong Democrat" to "strong Republican"; educational attainment; and demographic characteristics, such as gender, age, and racial identification.

The experiment itself is similar to the experimental design used in Chapter 4. Like the one used in Chapter 4, the experimental design I use here relies on the standard emotional recall technique in order to momentarily heighten individuals' level of anger. However, both the specific randomization strategy and the text of the induction technique that I employ here differ from the experiment in Chapter 4. While the previous experimental design employed an unconditional randomization, here I first block on individuals' self-identified partisan identification (obtained via the pre-experiment survey) and separately randomize the anger-induction within Democratic and Republican respondents.[7] The anger-induction technique differs from the one used in Chapter 4 in that, rather than asking individuals to recall a time they were "very angry" or "very angry about politics," here I ask individuals to recall a time they were very angry about the opposing political party and its supporters. Thus, Democratic respondents who were randomized into the treatment group were asked to write about a time they were very angry with the Republican Party and its supporters. Conversely, Republican respondents who were given the anger-inducing treatment were asked to write about a time they were very angry with the Democratic Party and its

---

[7] Those who identify as independents who lean toward one of the two parties are classified as partisans.

supporters.[8] Randomizing the treatment assignment within partisanship and eliciting this targeted anger is more appropriate than the design used in Chapter 4 because it better matches the theoretical expectation that anger will weaken citizens' commitment to democratic norms and values when it is directed specifically at the opposing political party. For both Democrats and Republicans, the control prompt asked individuals to write about what they ate for breakfast in the morning.

After the experimental manipulation participants were presented with one last battery of survey questions. Designed to assess individuals' support for democracy and democratic values, these prompts presented survey participants with a series of statements and asked them to rate their level of agreement with each. Agreement is measured on a 0–10 scale, where an answer of 0 indicates that the respondent "completely disagrees" with the statement and an answer of 10 indicates that the respondent "completely agrees" with the statement. Survey participants were shown the following statements:

1. In politics, the ends justify the means.
2. The Constitution often prevents my party from doing the things it wants to do.
3. The opposing party and its supporters are a threat to the country's well-being.
4. Those who hold different political views than me are less intelligent than I am.
5. Concern for minority opinions is slowing political progress in this country.
6. My party's elected officials tend to care too much about what the other party thinks.

The first two questions are designed to measure individuals' commitment to the democratic "rules of the game," which map onto what I have called the *functional definitions* of democracy. In a democratic setting, politicians and voters alike should be committed to upholding the established rules governing political competition and lawmaking. Yet, if anger is able to reduce one's commitment to this democratic norm, we should see those individuals who were randomized into the treatment group be more

---

[8] Because the experimental design randomizes the treatment assignment within partisan affiliation and focuses specifically on anger toward the opposing political party, individuals who self-identify as "pure independents" were dropped from the survey prior to the randomization stage.

likely to agree that "the ends justify the means" and that the Constitution tends to prevent his or her party from accomplishing its legislative and political goals.

Questions three and four tap into individuals' levels of political tolerance. Democratic theory argues that a party not in power should present itself as a "loyal opposition" to the governing party. That is, the party not in power is allowed to and – given the importance of vigorous political competition for the health of a democratic society – should present a set of policies that offer an alternative to those of the governing party while, at the same time, remaining loyal to the country, its institutions, and its political traditions. These questions assess the degree to which partisans are tolerant of the opposing party and its supporters acting as a legitimate and loyal opposition. If anger is able to weaken citizens' commitment to democratic norms and values, then those survey respondents who were randomized into the treatment condition should be more likely to believe that the opposing party and its supporters are a threat to the country's well-being and, as a more extreme measure, that those who hold different political views are of lesser intelligence.

Relatedly, the final two questions measure individuals' respect for minority opinions. One of the notable aspects of American government is its emphasis on protecting minority rights. As a particularly salient example, the institutional design of the Senate often requires supermajorities to pass legislation. Moreover, the Senate's institutional design has tended to facilitate more discussion and debate than most legislative bodies and, as a result, has earned the Senate the nickname of "the world's greatest deliberative body."[9] Such processes afford a considerable amount of time for minority opinions to be heard. However, if anger lowers individuals' commitment to the democratic norm of respecting minority opinions, then those who were randomized into the treatment group should be more likely to say that concern for minority opinions is slowing political progress in the country. These individuals should also be more likely to believe that their party's elected officials care too much about what the other party thinks.

Because the treatment intervention is randomized within individuals' stated partisanship, the effect of anger on citizens' commitment to democratic norms is estimated by subtracting the conditional expectation of

---

[9] Whether such a nickname is valid in an era of heightened polarization and gridlock is up for debate.

those in the control group from the conditional expectation of those in the treatment group. Formally, the average treatment effect (ATE) is:

$$E[Y \mid T = 1, P] - E[Y \mid T = 0, P] \qquad (5.1)$$

where Y is the outcome of interest (one of the six measures of democratic norms discussed above); $T = 1$ and $T = 0$ indicate individuals who were randomized into the treatment and control groups, respectively; and P denotes an individual's self-identified partisanship.

5.3.2 Results

Before proceeding to the results of the anger-induction experiment, it is useful to first examine the summary statistics for the data. Comprising 3,475 respondents, the sample is 56% Democrat and 44% Republican.[10] The sample is nearly balanced in terms of gender, with 48% identifying as male and the remaining 52% identifying as female. The sample is slightly more educated than the American public, with 38% of respondents indicating that they possess a bachelor's degree, a postgraduate degree, or some other professional degree. Just under 29% of the sample is non-White, which is only slightly more than the percentage of non-White individuals in the general public.

In addition to closely matching the sociodemographic makeup of the country, the sample is nicely divided between the treatment and control group. Table 5.1 presents balance statistics comparing the demographic and political profiles of those individuals who were randomized into the treatment group and those who were randomized into the control group. As can be seen, there are no statistically significant differences between the treated and control groups in terms of education, gender, racial identification or ideological leanings. Thus, the randomization process worked as intended.

The results of the treatment intervention suggest that anger does play a role in causing Americans to adopt attitudes that run counter to those one would expect in a healthy democratic society. These findings are most pronounced when examining the two questions meant to measure Americans' commitment to political tolerance. Compared to

---

[10] These numbers include those individuals who indicated that they are independents but lean toward one of the two parties.

TABLE 5.1 *Comparison of treated and control groups*

Variable	Treated	Control	Difference	P-Value
Bachelor's degree	0.37	0.39	−0.02	0.35
Male	0.47	0.49	−0.02	0.10
Non-White	0.29	0.28	0.01	0.44
Ideology	4.07	4.07	0.00	0.96

This table shows the balance between those individuals who were randomized into the treatment group and those who were randomized into the control group. The first three rows are proportions; the fourth row denotes the mean ideology score of respondents. There are no statistically significant differences between the two groups.

those who were randomized into the control group, those individuals who received the anger-inducing treatment were more likely to believe that the supporters of the opposing political party are a threat to the country's well-being ($\bar{y}_T - \bar{y}_C = .353; p < .001$). Similarly, receiving the anger-inducing treatment caused survey respondents to be more likely to agree with the idea that those who disagree with them politically are less intelligent than they are ($\bar{y}_T - \bar{y}_C = .192; p < .05$). Respondents who were randomized into the treatment group were also more likely to agree with the notion that concern for minority opinions is slowing political progress in the United States ($\bar{y}_T - \bar{y}_C = .192; p < .1$). The remaining three statements did not yield any difference between the treatment and control groups at any conventional level of statistical significance. Figure 5.2 plots the average treatment effect of anger on each dependent variable.[11]

The partisan differences in predicted level of agreement with these questions is illuminating. On average, Republicans were more likely than Democrats to agree with the statement that supporters of the opposing political party are a threat to the country's well-being. Republicans who were assigned to the control group gave an average response of 6.54 on the 0–10 scale; Republicans in the treatment group gave an average response of 6.80. By comparison, Democrats who were randomized into the control group gave an average response of 6.27. Democrats who received the anger-inducing treatment gave a response of 6.69.[12]

---

[11] Table 5.3 contains the regression estimates of each average treatment effect and can be found in the Appendix to this chapter.

[12] While the average response of treated Republicans on this metric is higher than that of treated Democrats, the difference between these two groups is not statistically significant at the 95% level.

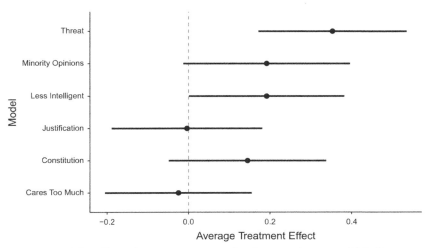

FIGURE 5.2. The effect of anger on support for democratic norms. This figure shows the average treatment effect of anger on each of the six democratic norms and values measured. The lines surrounding the treatment effects represent the 95% confidence intervals.

By contrast, Democrats were more likely than Republicans to say that those who disagree with them politically are less intelligent than they are. Republicans in the control group gave an average response of 2.75 on the 0–10 scale, while treated Republicans gave an average answer of 2.98. Democrats in the control group gave an average response of 3.15 to the question about political disagreements and intelligence. Democrats in the treated group gave a mean response of 3.31. Thus, in addition to expressing attitudes that run counter to the democratic ideal when made angry, there does appear to be a partisan difference in the ways in which these attitudes manifest themselves among the American public. Democrats are more likely to believe that Republicans are less intelligent than they are, while Republicans are more likely to endorse the belief that the political opposition poses a threat to the country's well-being.

5.3.3 Anger and the Institutional Structures of Democracy

The preceding results suggest that anger causes Americans to weaken in their commitment to democratic norms and values, particularly those norms and values pertaining to political tolerance and respect for minority opinions. Interestingly, however, anger does not appear to affect Americans' commitment to the institutional structures of democratic governance. Indeed, the results shown in Figure 5.2 indicate that anger had no effect on causing survey respondents to believe that the Constitution gets in the way of their party doing the things it wants to do or on endorsing the belief that the ends justify the means in politics. One potential reason for these null findings could be the nature of the questions that were used to measure Americans' commitment to the institutional structures of democratic government. As both of these measures are framed broadly, survey respondents might have had a difficult time assessing their level of agreement or disagreement with them. Moreover, it is possible that survey respondents were confused by the intent of these questions.

Therefore, in order to further examine the relationship between anger and Americans' commitment to the institutional structures of democracy, I conducted another experiment that sought to more directly test the effect of anger on citizens' attitudes toward democracy itself. Fielded via the Lucid Fulcrum academic platform, this experiment asked individuals to assess various aspects of democracies such as whether democracies are better than other forms of government and whether democracies produce efficient outcomes. The total sample size for the experiment is 2,649. As with the experiment in Section 5.3.2, I rely on the emotional recall technique to experimentally manipulate respondents' levels of anger. Thus, individuals who were randomized into the treatment group were asked to write about a time they were angry at the opposing political party, its leaders, or its supporters in the electorate. The control group was asked to write about a time they had thought about the opposing political party.[13] Similar to the experiment in Section 5.3.2, the assignment to one of these two randomization groups occurred separately among Democrats and Republicans. Treated and control units are balanced on the same metrics shown in Table 5.1.

After the randomization stage, respondents were asked a series of questions designed to measure commitment to the institutional structures of democracy. All questions were derived from Anderson et al.'s (2005) work on elections and perceptions of democratic legitimacy. One question, designed to measure "losers' consent," asked respondents

---

[13] This control prompt differs from the one used in the prior experiment. This prompt facilitates a more difficult comparison between treated and control units, as thinking about the opposing political party is likely to arouse some degree of anger. However, this control prompt offers a potentially cleaner experimental manipulation as the only difference between it and the treatment prompt is the presence of an anger-inducing cue.

TABLE 5.2 *Anger and democratic commitment*

	Elections Unfair (1)	Democratic Commitment (2)
Treated	0.008	−0.238
	(0.113)	(0.177)
Democrat	0.998***	1.287***
	(0.114)	(0.178)
Constant	5.399***	14.330***
	(0.101)	(0.156)
N	2,583	2,615
R^2	0.029	0.020

$^*p < .1$; $^{**}p < .05$; $^{***}p < .01$.
This table shows the effect of anger on Americans' commitment to the institutional structures of democracy.

their perceptions about whether the most recent election in the United States was conducted fairly or unfairly, with higher values indicating a greater belief that the most recent election was *not* conducted fairly. Other questions asked respondents to indicate the extent to which they agree that having a democratic political system is a good thing for a society; whether democracies, in spite of their problems, are better than other forms of government; whether democracies produce efficient economies; whether democracies are indecisive and prone to "too much squabbling"; whether democracies are good at maintaining order; and, finally, whether other forms of government – such as having a "strong leader," a technocratic ruling class, or military rule – would be appropriate ways to run the country. These questions are then combined into an additive scale, ranging from 0 to 24, where higher values indicate a greater commitment to the institutional structures of democracy.[14] The results, shown in Table 5.2, suggest that anger does not cause citizens to weaken in their commitment to the institutional structures of democracy.

As shown in Table 5.2, anger neither increases the belief that elections are conducted unfairly (column one) nor does it lower individuals' overall commitment to the institutional structures of democratic governance (column two). These results corroborate the null findings in Section 5.3.2 with regard to anger and perceptions that the Constitution prevents one's party from doing the things it wants to do and the belief that, in politics, the

---

[14] The full text of the questions used can be found in the Appendix.

ends justify the means. Additionally, these results provide an important context for the claims in this chapter. While anger can and does lower citizens' commitment to specific democratic norms and values, particularly those focusing on political tolerance and respect for minority opinions, it does not cause Americans to want to abandon democracy as a whole. In this sense, the effects of anger appear to be limited to what I referred to in Section 5.1 as the indicators of a liberal democracy. What I have referred to as the "functional" aspects of democracy, or the institutional structures of democracy, appear to be immune to the deleterious effects of mass-level anger.

5.4 CONCLUSION AND DISCUSSION

The results I have presented in this chapter indicate that anger is a partial cause of Americans' weakening commitment to democratic norms and values. Specifically, anger appears to attenuate Americans' connection to democratic norms and values mainly by lowering individuals' levels of political tolerance. When Democrats or Republicans are made angry specifically at the opposing political party, its leaders, or its supporters in the electorate, they are more likely to agree with two anti-democratic statements: that supporters of the opposing political party are a threat to the country's well-being and that those who disagree with them politically are less intelligent than they are.

However, it is important to note that the effect of anger on democratic commitment has its limits. Anger does not appear to cause Americans to weaken in their commitment to what I have called the functional aspects of democracy (e.g., respect for the codified "rules of the game"), or the institutional structures of democracy. That anger does not cause citizens to want to abandon democratic governance is encouraging. Yet, there remains substantial evidence that anger lowers citizens' devotions to key aspects of a liberal democracy. The implications of such a finding are vast. In an ideal democratic setting citizens should be able to articulate differences over policy preferences and do so while recognizing the opposing side's legitimacy. Moreover, these differences should not spill over to apolitical evaluations. The results I have presented in this chapter suggest that anger violates this key tenet of liberal democracy. Indeed, when Americans are angry their differences transcend politics or public policy and directly affect evaluations of the personal worth of those who hold different political opinions. Operating via the mechanism of appraisal theory (Roseman, Spindel, and Jose 1990), anger causes

Americans to judge and evaluate their fellow citizens' worth through the prism of political beliefs.

This inability to separate a person's political preferences from their intelligence or their relationship to the country's well-being does not portend well for the future of deliberation in the United States. Good governance requires a delicate balance of give-and-take between the two major political parties. When the supporters of these parties in the electorate increasingly view those on the other side of the political divide as harmful to the country's well-being and less intelligent than themselves, elected officials will be constrained in their ability to negotiate in good faith with their political opponents due to the passions and desires of their electoral bases. Such a constraint is unlikely to be loosened so long as Democrats and Republicans in the electorate are unable to separate personal evaluations from political beliefs. With anger continuing to play a large role in the American political arena, the connection between the personal and the political is unlikely to abate.

5.5 APPENDIX

5.5.1 Experiment #1

Survey Questions
- In what year were you born?
- Are you male or female?
- Which of the following race or ethnic groups do you most identify with?

  – White, non-Hispanic
  – Black, non-Hispanic
  – Asian, native Hawaiian, or other Pacific Islander
  – Native American
  – Hispanic
  – Other

- What is your highest level of educational attainment?

  – High school graduate or G.E.D.
  – Some college but no degree
  – Associates degree
  – Bachelor's degree
  – Postgraduate degree
  – Professional degree

- Where would you place yourself on the following party identification scale?

  - Strong Democrat
  - Weak Democrat
  - Independent but lean Democrat
  - Independent but lean Republican
  - Weak Republican
  - Strong Republican

- Where would you rate yourself on the following political ideology scale?

  - Very liberal
  - Liberal
  - Slightly liberal
  - Moderate; middle of the road
  - Slightly conservative
  - Conservative
  - Very conservative

- On a "feeling thermometer" scale from 0 to 100, where 0 indicates the coldest possible rating, 50 represents neutral, and 100 represents the warmest possible rating, how would you rate the following groups?

  - The Democratic Party
  - The Republican Party

Experimental Manipulations
Treatment Group. Block on party: *Please write a short paragraph about a time you were very angry at the (Democratic/Republican) Party, its leaders, or its supporters in the electorate. Be sure to describe precisely how this experience made you feel so that someone else reading it might also become angry.*

Control Group. Please write about what you ate for breakfast in the morning.

Post-experiment
Please rate your level of agreement with the following statements on a 0–10 scale, where 0 indicates that you agree "not at all" and 10 indicates that you agree "completely."

   1. The opposing party and its supporters are a threat to the country's well-being.

2. Those who hold different political views than me are less intelligent than I am.
3. In politics, the ends justify the means.
4. The Constitution often prevents my party from doing the things it wants to do.
5. Concern for minority opinions is slowing political progress in this country.
6. My party's elected officials tend to care too much about what the other party thinks.

The Effect of Anger on Democratic Norms and Values

The results from Table 5.3 were used to produce Figure 5.2.

5.5.2 Experiment #2

Survey Questions
Experimental Manipulations

Treatment Group. Block on party: *Please write a short paragraph about a time you were very angry at the (Democratic/Republican) Party, its leaders, or its supporters in the electorate. Be sure to describe precisely how this experience made you feel so that someone else reading it might also become angry.*

Control Group. Please write about a time you thought about the opposing political party, its leaders, or its supporters in the electorate.

Post-experiment

- In some countries, people believe their elections are conducted fairly. In other countries, people believe that their elections are conducted unfairly. Thinking of the last election in the United States, where would you place it on this scale of 1–10, where 1 means that the last election was conducted fairly and 10 means that the election was conducted unfairly?
- Would you say that having a democratic political system is a very good, fairly good, fairly bad, or very bad way of governing this country? Very good (3); fairly good (2); fairly bad (1); very bad (0).
- Could you please tell me if you agree strongly, agree, disagree, or disagree strongly with the following statement: "Democracy may have problems but it's better than any other form of government." Agree strongly (3); agree (2); disagree (1); disagree strongly (0).

TABLE 5.3 *The causal effect of anger on democratic norms and values*

	Threat	Less Intelligent	Justification	Constitution Prevents	Minority Opinions	Care Too Much
Treated	0.353***	0.192**	-0.004	0.144	0.192*	-0.025
	(0.093)	(0.097)	(0.094)	(0.099)	(0.104)	(0.092)
Democrat	-0.200**	0.371***	0.031	0.589***	-1.251***	-0.338***
	(0.093)	(0.098)	(0.095)	(0.099)	(0.105)	(0.092)
Constant	6.498***	2.768***	4.021***	3.412***	5.106***	5.441***
	(0.082)	(0.086)	(0.084)	(0.088)	(0.093)	(0.082)
N	3,453	3,467	3,460	3,462	3,457	3,461
R^2	0.006	0.005	0.00003	0.011	0.041	0.004

$*p < .1; **p < .05; ***p < .01.$

This table shows the effect of anger on support for various democratic norms and values. In particular, anger causes citizens to be more likely to believe that supporters of the opposing political party are a threat to the country's well-being, and that those that disagree with them politically are less intelligent than they are.

- I'm going to list some things that people sometimes say about a democratic political system. Could you please tell me if you agree strongly, agree, disagree, or disagree strongly, after I list each one? Agree strongly (0); agree (1); disagree (2); disagree strongly (3).

  - In a democracy, the economic system runs badly.
  - Democracies are indecisive and have too much squabbling.
  - Democracies aren't good at maintaining order.

- I'm going to describe various types of political systems and ask what you think about each as a way of governing this country. For each one, would you say it is a very good, fairly good, fairly bad, or very bad way of governing this country? Very good (0); fairly good (1); fairly bad (2); very bad (3).

  - Having a strong leader who does not have to bother with Congress and elections?
  - Having experts, not the government, make decisions according to what they think is best for the country?
  - Having the army rule the country?

6

Anger and Voter Loyalty

If a man be under the influence of anger his conduct will not be correct.
— Confucius

Thus far I have argued that anger has the ability to lower Americans' trust in their government and, furthermore, to weaken the public's commitment to democratic norms and values. Additionally, in Chapter 2 I argued that political elites strategically elicit mass-level anger toward the opposing political party and its supporters. Yet, these findings present a puzzle: if anger has deleterious consequences for effective governance and democratic values, why do political elites continue to stoke anger among their followers? In this chapter I argue that the resolution to this paradox lies in political elites' electoral desires. More specifically, I argue that political elites are content with bearing the negative externalities of arousing the public's anger because this anger serves to solidify partisan loyalty. This partisan loyalty, in turn, bolsters elites' electoral fortunes.

To illustrate how anger leads to voter loyalty I utilize data from the 2016 American National Election Studies (ANES). I show that, regardless of how Americans felt about their own party and their own party's presidential candidate along a 0–100 "feeling thermometer" scale, those individuals who were most frequently angry at the opposing party's presidential candidate were the most likely to vote for their own party's presidential candidate. In fact, anger's ability to produce party loyalty is most pronounced among those individuals who view their own party's candidate either negatively or neutrally on this feeling thermometer scale. Given the fact that the 2016 presidential election featured the two most unpopular candidates in the country's history (Collins 2016; Saad 2016), the fact that anger was nevertheless able to produce such high degrees of partisan loyalty is striking.

I then build on these findings to show how anger works in forging partisan loyalty in the context of a nationalized political system. Using data on 2016 Congressional election outcomes, I show that those individuals who were more frequently angry at the opposing party's presidential candidate were more likely to vote for their own party's candidates for the US Senate and House of Representatives. As with the results I present regarding anger and presidential loyalty, the results pertaining to anger and voter loyalty in subpresidential elections are most pronounced for those who have poor affective evaluations of their own party's candidates. The results indicate that, in the contemporary political environment characterized by a high degree of nationalization, anger works as a partisan bonding agent at all levels of the federal electoral system.

To begin, I briefly discuss the 2016 election and the anger it often elicited among the mass public. I then develop a theory as to why politicians stoke anger among the public even though, as I have shown in previous chapters, higher levels of anger have deleterious consequences for citizens' trust in government and commitment to democratic norms and values. Arguing that anger produces partisan loyalty, I present a series of empirical results showing that individuals who more frequently feel angry toward the opposing party's presidential candidate are more loyal to their own party in Presidential, House, and Senate elections.

6.1 THE 2016 US PRESIDENTIAL ELECTION

As discussed in Chapter 2, the 2016 US Presidential Election was, above all else, anger-inducing. Contested by Hillary Clinton, the Democratic candidate, and Donald Trump, the Republican candidate, the campaign season was described by the electorate as a "mess," "frightening," "worrisome," and "unique" (PBS 2016).

Though the 2016 election was unique in many ways, it certainly was not the only election in American history that caused the electorate to become angry. Indeed, from 1980 – when the ANES first began asking the question – to 2012 the mean percentage of respondents who reported ever feeling angry at the opposing party's presidential candidate is 56%. Such a high number reflects the fact that politicians have long sought to arouse anger among the mass public and that Americans have a history of fighting over contentious political issues. What was unique about the 2016 election – in addition to the unpopularity of the two major party candidates – was the *degree* to which Americans expressed their anger toward the opposing party's candidates.

In comparison to the 2012 election, which was contentious in its own right, the 2016 election saw a large increase in the percentage of Americans who reported feeling angry at the opposing party's presidential candidate "always" or "most of the time." In 2012, 50.7% of Democrats and 50.1% of Republicans reported these high frequencies of anger toward the opposing party's presidential candidate. Four years later, these numbers had jumped to 69.6% and 64.3%, respectively. This represents a 37.3% increase among Democrats and a 28.3% increase among Republicans.

Such increases almost surely had to do with the nature of the campaign itself. Trump's campaign was notable for his massive rallies, a percentage of which resulted in physical violence – sometimes with encouragement from the candidate himself.[1] Indeed, during one rally Trump famously offered to pay the legal fees of any of his supporters who were charged with assault while removing counterprotesters. Such anger and charged partisan rhetoric culminated in the cancellation of a planned Trump rally in Chicago after a massive protest resulted in skirmishes between pro- and anti-Trump mobs, leading to a handful of injuries and arrests.[2]

Clinton, for her part, went to great lengths to portray Trump as historically unfit for the office of the presidency. Portraying his policies as "dark" and "divisive," Clinton frequently told her supporters that Trump was "dangerously incoherent" and petulant (Krieg 2016; Lee and Merica 2016). After Trump's inauguration, this building Democratic anger would translate into a series of nationwide protests that came to be known as the "Women's March" and "The Resistance."

6.2 WHY STOKE ANGER?

As argued in Chapter 2 and shown in the above synopsis of the 2016 presidential campaign, politicians frequently seek to invoke anger among their supporters. The question left unanswered is simple: why do politicians

---

[1] For example, see this report from *The Washington Post*: www.washingtonpost.com/news/the-fix/wp/2017/04/03/the-violent-rally-trump-cant-move-past/.

[2] See this CNN report for more information: www.cnn.com/2016/03/11/politics/donald-trump-chicago-protests/.

do this? As Grimmer (2013) notes, "partisan taunting" is a key aspect of being a politician. Thus, according to Grimmer (2013), such taunting is simply part and parcel of running for office – especially for those politicians in electorally safe districts or states. Yet, while Grimmer's (2013) analysis is a groundbreaking study in the field of political communication, the precise reasoning as to *why* politicians engage in "partisan taunting" is unclear. While such taunting certainly serves to remind a politician's constituents of his or her partisan identification, as Grimmer (2013) notes, I argue that partisan taunting does more than simply highlight a politician's partisan leanings. Indeed, I contend that partisan taunting is done deliberately and strategically because it invokes anger among the politician's base toward the party or candidate that is being taunted. This anger, in turn, forges partisan loyalty. Put succinctly, an angry voter is a loyal voter.

One reason that angry voters are loyal voters has to do with the psychological effects of anger itself. Bodenhausen, Sheppard, and Kramer (1994) show that anger increases the use of group stereotypes and other heuristics, leading angry people to be "more likely to rely on simple cues in reacting to social stimuli." To provide evidence for this claim, Bodenhausen, Sheppard, and Kramer (1994) ran an experiment that sought to determine the ways in which negative emotions (such as anger or sadness) affected individuals' perceptions of guilt in their peers who, in one scenario, were accused of assault, and, in another scenario, were accused of cheating on an academic test. In some cases, participants were also told that the individual was Hispanic ("Juan Garcia") or not Hispanic ("John Garner"). Moreover, some participants were told that the accused individual participated in campus athletics, while others were not given this information. Bodenhausen, Sheppard, and Kramer (1994) hypothesized that experiment participants would, stereotypically, be more likely to believe that the individual with the Hispanic surname was guilty of assault than the individual with the non-Hispanic surname, and that the athlete was more likely to be guilty of academic fraud than the nonathlete. The results of this experiment confirmed that participants who were given an anger-inducing stimulus were more likely to believe that the stereotypically accused individuals were guilty (i.e., the Hispanic accused of assault and the athlete accused of cheating) than those who were given a sadness-inducing stimulus or no emotional prompt at all.

Follow-up experiments by these same authors found that anger does more than increase reliance on group stereotypes. In fact, two more experiments found that individuals who were put into an angry state were more

likely to agree with expert opinions and more likely to agree with statements made by individuals who are perceived to be trustworthy. Thus,
anger has been shown to increase reliance on cues or preconceived notions
across multiple studies. Because partisanship is the most salient cue in
American politics, individuals who are angry should be more likely to rely
on their partisan identities to guide their voting behavior. Moreover, they
should be more receptive to in-party elite rhetoric. Both of these anger-
induced behaviors are expected to lead to greater levels of party loyalty
at the ballot box.

In addition to its psychological effects, experiencing anger can lead to
voter loyalty by priming an individual to exhibit higher degrees of negative partisanship. The phenomenon whereby individuals are motivated to
vote not *for* their own party but *against* the opposing party (Abramowitz
and Webster 2016), negative partisanship is a strong predictor of voter
loyalty and is likely connected to multiple negative emotions. That is,
individuals who dislike the opposing political party may do so out of
fear, anxiety, disgust, anger, or some other negatively valenced emotion.
To provide evidence that anger triggers negative partisanship, I begin by
creating a measure designed to replicate the Abramowitz and Webster
(2016) notion of "negative partisanship." This measure captures the relative degree of dislike and like of one's own party and the opposing party. It
is calculated by using the feeling thermometer ratings toward the Democratic and Republican parties included in the 2016 ANES. Frequently
used in studies of political behavior, the ANES feeling thermometer
ratings range from 0 to 100. A score of zero is the lowest evaluation that
an individual can give a party, while a score of 100 is the highest.

To create the measure of "negative partisanship," I first subtract an
individual's feeling thermometer rating of the opposing party from 100.
Next, I subtract that same individual's rating of their own party from this
first calculation. Thus, the measure of negative partisanship is:

$$(100 - \text{Other party F.T.}) - \text{Own party F.T.} \qquad (6.1)$$

This variable ranges from -100 to 100. By construction, negative values indicate that the respondent likes their own party more than they
dislike the opposing party. On the other hand, positive values on this
measure indicate that an individual dislikes the opposing party more than
they like their own party. Any individual who scores a positive value on
this metric is classified as a negative partisan.[3]

---

[3] This measure is adopted from Webster (2018*b*).

Simple bivariate statistics suggest that anger is a commonly felt emotion among those individuals who are negative partisans. Indeed, among those who are classified as negative partisans by the metric shown in Equation 6.1, 83% reported that they felt angry toward the opposing party's presidential candidate "about half the time" or more. Nearly as many – 74% – reported feeling angry at the opposing party's presidential candidate "most of the time" or "always." Figure 6.1 shows the percentage of time that individuals felt angry at the opposing party's presidential candidate.

While the data shown in Figure 6.1 is suggestive of a link between negative affect toward the opposing party and anger, it is only preliminary. To more definitively establish a link between negative partisanship and anger, I present linear probability models that regress an indicator of negative partisanship status (1 = negative partisan, 0 = not) on the frequency with which individuals reported feeling angry at the opposing party's presidential candidate. This regression output is displayed in the first column in Table 6.1. In the second column, I include controls for an individual's age, gender, race, and level of education. The third column includes an additional control for self-reported ideology.

Across all three model specifications, more frequently feeling angry at the opposing party's presidential candidate is associated with a higher probability of being a negative partisan. The coefficient becomes larger in magnitude when controls for demographics and a measure of ideology are added. In all three specifications, the coefficient estimate is statistically significant at the $p < .01$ level. While these models do not assess the direction of causality, they nevertheless suggest the existence of a strong connection between feeling angry at the opposing party's presidential candidate and being a negative partisan. Thus, by stoking anger among the electorate, political elites are increasing the probability that an individual will identify as a negative partisan and remain loyal to one's own party.

6.3 ANGRY VOTERS, LOYAL VOTERS

To illustrate the role of anger in forging partisan loyalty I utilized data from the 2016 ANES. Key for this analysis is an indicator of whether or not an individual voted loyally for their own party's presidential candidate. Democrats, including independents who reported leaning toward the Democratic Party, were coded as voting loyally if they voted

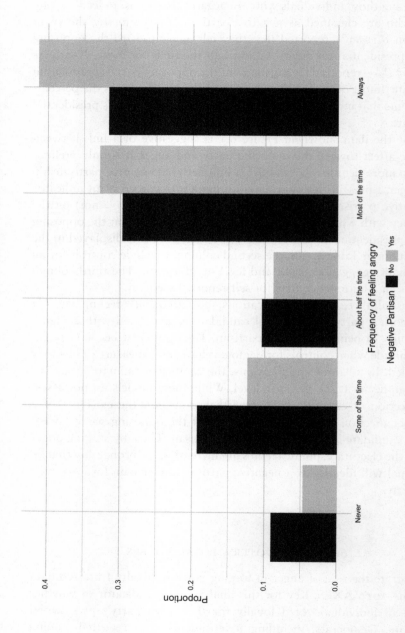

FIGURE 6.1. Negative partisans and anger at opposing party candidates. This figure shows the proportion of individuals, broken down by negative partisanship status, that experienced each frequency of anger at the opposing party's presidential candidate.

Data come from the 2016 American National Election Studies.

TABLE 6.1 *The relationship between anger and negative partisanship*

	Negative Partisan		
Anger	0.058***	0.058***	0.062***
	(0.007)	(0.007)	(0.009)
Demographics	No	Yes	Yes
Ideology	No	No	Yes
N	3,605	3,450	2,788

$*p < .1; **p < .05; ***p < .01.$
This table shows the relationship between the frequency of feeling angry toward the opposing party's candidate and negative partisanship. There is a close and robust relationship between the two, suggesting that anger is a key part of negative partisanship.

for Hillary Clinton. Similarly, Republicans, including independents who reported leaning toward the Republican Party, were coded as voting loyally if they voted for Donald Trump. Third-party voters and candidates were removed from the analysis.

To examine the nature of loyal voting during the 2016 election, I regressed the partisan loyalty measure described above on measures of anger, partisan affect, and partisan strength. The anger measure is operationalized by how frequently individuals reported feeling angry toward the opposing party's presidential candidate. The partisan affect variables are measured by feeling thermometer ratings toward one's own party and one's own party's candidates for elected office. Finally, the partisan strength variable is a dummy variable that equals one if an individual reported being a "strong partisan" on the 7-point partisan identification scale.[4] In column two I also include a control variable for anxiety, operationalized by how frequently individuals reported feeling fearful or anxious toward the opposing party's presidential candidate. To facilitate ease of comparison, all of the independent variables have been scaled to range from 0 to 1. Estimation is via logistic regression. The results of these models are shown in Table 6.2.[5]

The most important predictor of whether an individual votes loyally for her own party's presidential candidate is how she feels, on an affective dimension, toward her own party's candidate. However, because the

---

[4] This captures both individuals who identify as "strong Democrats" and "strong Republicans."
[5] This model replicates the one found in Abramowitz and Webster (2018a).

TABLE 6.2 *Angry voters, loyal voters*

	Vote Loyally	
	(1)	(2)
Anger	4.889***	4.087***
	(0.459)	(0.611)
Anxiety		1.326**
		(0.592)
FT own party	0.687	0.715
	(0.744)	(0.740)
FT own party candidate	5.958***	5.742***
	(0.579)	(0.579)
Strong partisan	1.122***	1.101***
	(0.388)	(0.378)
Constant	−3.519***	−3.678***
	(0.404)	(0.417)
N	2,248	2,247
Log likelihood	−286.149	−279.394
AIC	582.298	570.788

*p < .1; **p < .05; ***p < .01.
This table presents results from a logistic regression showing the relationship between anger at the opposing party's presidential candidate and voting loyally at the presidential level. Higher levels of anger are associated with a higher likelihood of voting loyally.

feeling thermometer measures on the ANES do not reveal *why* individuals give the ratings that they do, it is difficult to say whether this measure is driven by feelings of optimism, hope, or some other quality in their own party's presidential candidate that appeals to a voter. Regardless of the precise nature, however, the results in Table 6.2 suggest that how individuals feel about their own party's presidential candidate is of the utmost importance for loyal voting.

Outside of the feeling thermometer measure toward the in-party candidate, the most important factor in predicting partisan loyalty is anger toward the opposing party's candidate. The positive coefficient indicates that more frequently feeling angry toward the opposing party's candidate is associated with a higher likelihood of voting loyally for one's own party's candidate. The strength of this relationship is quite impressive: it is nearly on par with feeling thermometer ratings of the in-party candidate, and it vastly outperforms feeling thermometer ratings of the in-party and an indicator for whether an individual identifies as a "strong partisan."

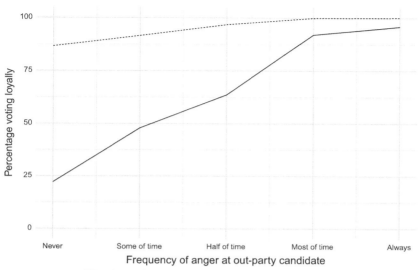

FIGURE 6.2. Anger forges partisan loyalty. This figure shows the percentage of individuals who voted loyally for their own party's presidential candidate as anger toward the opposing party's candidate increases.

Moreover, anger remains a statistically significant predictor of voter loyalty even when controlling for anxiety.

Yet, while anger toward the opposing party's presidential candidate is an important predictor of loyalty in the unconditional regression shown in Table 6.2, the importance of anger as a way of forging partisan loyalty is most clearly seen when examining the interactive relationship between anger and feelings toward the in-party presidential candidate. To illustrate the differential effects of anger toward the opposing party's presidential candidate by feelings toward the in-party candidate, I created a dummy variable indicating whether an individual felt positive toward their own party's candidate or negative.[6] I then calculated the percentage of individuals who voted loyally for their party's presidential candidate within each of these groups as the frequency of anger toward the opposing party's presidential candidate increases. These calculations are displayed graphically in Figure 6.2.

---

[6] Those who felt neutral toward their own party's presidential candidate were included in the "negative" category.

These results indicate that, for those who felt positive toward their own party's presidential candidate, anger toward the opposing party's presidential candidate played a minimal role in predicting partisan loyalty. In fact, among those individuals who liked their own party's candidate and reported never feeling angry toward the opposing party's presidential candidate, 86.6% voted loyally. This percentage increases monotonically as anger toward the opposing party's presidential candidate increases.

Though anger plays a small role in forging partisan loyalty for those individuals who like their own party's candidate, its real strength lies in its ability to make those who do not like their own party's presidential candidate nevertheless look like rabid partisans. Among those individuals who did not like their own party's presidential candidate and reported never feeling angry toward the opposing party's presidential candidate, only 22% cast a loyal vote. Among those individuals who did not like their own party's presidential candidate but indicated that they felt angry at the opposing party's candidate "some of the time," 47.7% voted loyally. When the frequency of anger toward the opposing party's presidential candidate increases to "half of the time," the percentage of loyal voters increases to 63.6%. The biggest jump comes when individuals who did not like their own party's candidate reported feeling angry at the opposing party's candidate "most of the time." Among these individuals, 92% voted loyally for their own party's candidate. Finally, for those who reported "always" feeling angry at the opposing party's candidate, 95.8% voted loyally for their own party's presidential candidate.

6.4 ANGER AND VOTER LOYALTY IN A NATIONALIZED ENVIRONMENT

In addition to its ability to forge partisan loyalty at the presidential level, it is also likely that anger toward the opposing party's presidential candidate leads to voter loyalty in subpresidential elections. Such an expectation is rooted in the growing amount of evidence that suggests that American politics and elections in the contemporary era are increasingly "nationalized" (see, e.g., Abramowitz and Webster 2016; Hopkins 2018). That is, rather than being contested over local and state issues as the Framers of the US Constitution intended, elections for the US House of Representatives and the Senate are fought over national issues.

According to Hopkins (2018), one reason that voting patterns in the United States are nationalized is due to the strategic choices candidates make while campaigning. Candidates routinely invoke national issues while campaigning because they tend to be highly salient and encourage participation. These national issues also serve to trigger partisan cues that guide voting decisions. This trend toward nationalized candidate behavior is perpetuated by an easier access to diverse media outlets, which has pushed citizens toward a greater consumption of national instead of local news. As Hopkins (2018) notes, "someone waking up in Oklahoma City in 1930 could not expect to read that day's *Los Angeles Times*." With the change in the media landscape and the growth of the Internet, as discussed in Chapter 1, this is no longer the case. This ease of access to a wide range of newspapers has altered the media's incentives toward an increase in the amount of national news they produce and a decrease in the amount of state and local news they produce.

The ability of the news media to nationalize American political competition and voting behavior has been most cogently articulated by Martin and McCrain (2018), who studied the acquisition patterns and effects of the Sinclair Broadcast Group. Their analysis suggests that Sinclair's pattern of station acquisition is largely motivated by increasing their market share and expanding their geographic coverage. While Sinclair's acquisition strategy is what would be expected of any business, the downstream effects of Sinclair's growing media empire is worrisome. Martin and McCrain (2018) show that, when a TV station is acquired by Sinclair, it devotes significantly less time to local issues and much more time to national political issues.[7] With Sinclair's market share potentially increasing to 72% of American households, pending the completion of the purchase of a rival company, the nationalized political environment of contemporary American politics is unlikely to go away any time soon.

Given the trend toward nationalization in American politics, understanding how voter anger at the presidential level shapes voting patterns at subpresidential levels is essential. To do this, I once again utilize data from the 2016 ANES. As with the results presented in Table 6.2, the key independent variable in this analysis is the frequency with which respondents felt angry at the opposing party's presidential candidate. However, unlike the model of presidential loyalty, the analysis here uses two dependent variables: the first measures partisan loyalty in House elections, while

---

[7] The study also suggests that TV stations acquired by Sinclair shift the coverage of their tone to the ideological right.

TABLE 6.3 Anger and partisan loyalty in subpresidential elections

	Vote Loyally		Vote Loyally	
	House (1)	House (2)	Senate (3)	Senate (4)
Anger	0.941***	0.610	1.704***	1.432**
	(0.347)	(0.449)	(0.485)	(0.557)
Anxiety		0.484		0.446
		(0.428)		(0.419)
FT own party	−1.050*	−1.094*	0.515	0.496
	(0.630)	(0.629)	(0.844)	(0.839)
FT own party candidate	5.790***	5.803***	8.324***	8.346***
	(0.816)	(0.804)	(1.484)	(1.495)
Strong partisan	0.257	0.245	0.428	0.387
	(0.253)	(0.255)	(0.336)	(0.336)
Constant	−1.485***	−1.542***	−4.574***	−4.641***
	(0.549)	(0.540)	(0.767)	(0.768)
N	1,658	1,658	1,291	1,290
Log likelihood	−490.618	−489.875	−335.471	−330.977
AIC	991.236	991.750	680.942	673.954

$^*p < .1$; $^{**}p < .05$; $^{***}p < .01$.
These results show that anger toward the opposing party's presidential candidate predicts partisan loyalty in subpresidential elections.

the second measures partisan loyalty in Senate elections (1 = loyal, 0 = not loyal). In order to minimize the bias in my estimates, I also include control variables for feeling thermometer ratings of the respondent's own party and the respondent's own party's candidate (which, depending on the model, captures feeling thermometer ratings toward the in-party House candidate or the in-party Senate candidate). As with the model in Table 6.2, I also include a dummy variable for whether or not an individual identifies as a strong partisan. The models displayed in columns two and four also contain control variables for anxiety. All variables are scaled to range from 0 to 1 for ease of interpretation. As with the model predicting partisan loyalty at the presidential level, the models predicting loyalty at the subpresidential level are estimated via logistic regression. These results are shown in Table 6.3.

The results of the models displayed in Table 6.3 are remarkably similar to the models predicting partisan loyalty at the presidential level. As with the models of presidential loyalty, the results of the models displayed in Table 6.3 indicate that the most important factor in predicting partisan loyalty in House and Senate elections is how an individual rates their own party's House or Senate candidate on the feeling thermometer score. Higher affective ratings on this scale are associated with a higher likelihood of voting loyally for one's own party's candidates.

However, as with the results examining presidential loyalty, the results shown in Table 6.3 suggest that, in an era of nationalization, anger toward the opposing party's presidential candidate is predictive of voter loyalty in subpresidential elections. This relationship is robust to the inclusion of a measure of anxiety in models predicting voter loyalty in Senate elections; however, anger fails to reach any conventional level of statistical significance when controlling for anxiety in the model predicting voter loyalty in House elections. One potential explanation for why anger continues to operate in this more fully specified model in Senate but not House elections is that Senate elections are, by definition, statewide races that often receive higher media attention and are therefore more susceptible to the growing trends of nationalization than elections for the House of Representatives (Hopkins 2018).

As with the model predicting voter loyalty in presidential elections, the ability of anger to forge partisan loyalty in subpresidential elections is greatest for those individuals who hold negative or neutral affective evaluations of their own party's candidates. Figure 6.3 shows the relationship between frequency of anger toward the opposing party's presidential candidate and voting loyally for one's own party in House elections, broken out by affective ratings toward one's own party's House candidate.

For those individuals who view their own party's House candidate positively, anger plays a minimal role in increasing partisan loyalty. Indeed, for those individuals who liked their own party's House candidate and reported never feeling angry at the opposing party's presidential candidate, 93.1% voted loyally for their own party. For those individuals who liked their own party's House candidate and reported "always" feeling angry at the opposing party's presidential candidate, 93.9% voted loyally for their own party's House candidate. This small difference between the lowest level and the highest level of anger toward the opposing party's presidential candidate suggests that, for those individuals who viewed their own party's House candidate favorably, anger does little to produce partisan loyalty in House elections.

While anger appears to play a limited role in producing voter loyalty in House elections for those who liked their own party's House candidate, it was much more effective in producing voter loyalty among those who did not particularly like their own party's candidate. As shown in Figure 6.3,

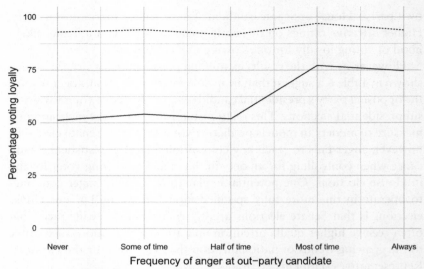

FIGURE 6.3. Anger and voter loyalty in House elections. This figure shows the relationship between anger at the opposing party's presidential candidate and voting loyally in House elections. The relationship between anger and voter loyalty in House elections is most pronounced for those individuals who hold negative or neutral views of their own party's House candidate.

those individuals who did not like their own party's House candidate and reported never feeling angry at the opposing party's presidential candidate were almost equally as likely to vote for their party's House candidate as they were to vote for the opposing party's House candidate. Indeed, among these individuals, only 51.3% cast a loyal vote. By contrast, for those individuals who did not like their own party's House candidate but reported feeling angry at the opposing party's presidential candidate "most of the time" or "always," approximately 75% voted loyally for their own party. Thus, as with the relationship between anger and voter loyalty at the presidential level, more frequently feeling angry toward the opposing party's presidential candidate makes those individuals who disliked their own party's House candidate look much more like dedicated partisans.

A similar pattern – shown in Figure 6.4 – emerges with Senate elections. Among those individuals who liked their own party's Senate candidate and reported never feeling angry toward the opposing party's presidential candidate, 76.3% voted loyally for their own party's Senate candidate.

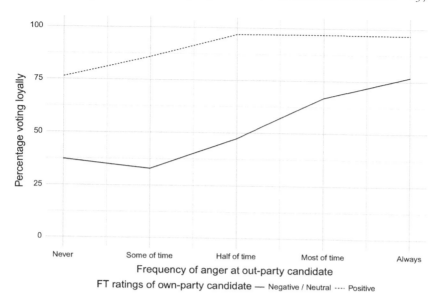

FIGURE 6.4. Anger and voter loyalty in Senate elections. This figure shows the relationship between anger at the opposing party's presidential candidate and voting loyally in Senate elections. The relationship between anger and voter loyalty in Senate elections is most pronounced for those individuals who hold negative or neutral views of their own party's Senate candidate.

Ninety-seven percent of individuals who liked their own party's Senate candidate and reported feeling angry toward the opposing party's presidential candidate "half of the time" voted loyally for their own party. The percentage of individuals voting loyally remained the same among those who liked their own party's Senate candidate and reported feeling angry at the opposing party's presidential candidate "most of the time" or "always." The magnitude of these changes indicates that, for those individuals who liked their own party's candidate, anger played a larger role in forging partisan loyalty in Senate elections than in House elections.

While the relationship between anger and voting loyally among those who liked their own party's candidate looks different for Senate elections than it does for presidential or House races, a familiar pattern exists among those individuals who did not like their own party's Senate candidate. Among those individuals who did not like their own party's Senate candidate and reported never feeling angry at the opposing party's presidential candidate, only 37.3% voted loyally for their party's candidate. Among the category of respondents who reported feeling angry at the

TABLE 6.4 *Anger and consistently loyal voters*

	Consistent Voter Loyalty	
	(1)	(2)
Anger	1.498***	1.134***
	(0.307)	(0.388)
Anxiety		0.563
		(0.364)
FT own party	−0.323	−0.319
	(0.589)	(0.595)
FT own party candidate	2.022***	1.932***
	(0.473)	(0.482)
Strong partisan	0.467**	0.459**
	(0.197)	(0.198)
Constant	−1.233***	−1.290***
	(0.318)	(0.316)
N	1,157	1,157
Log likelihood	−609.515	−608.160
AIC	1,229.031	1,228.319

$^*p < .1$; $^{**}p < .05$; $^{***}p < .01$.
This table shows the relationship between voter anger and voting
consistently for one's own party's slate of candidates at the
presidential, House, and Senate levels.

opposing party's presidential candidate "most of the time," nearly 67%
voted loyally for their own party's Senate candidate. Finally, nearly 77%
of those individuals who did not like their own party's Senate candidate
but reported "always" feeling angry at the opposing party's presidential
candidate voted loyally.

The preceding results indicate that anger can lead to voter loyalty
in presidential, House, and Senate elections. However, one unanswered
question pertains to whether or not anger is able to push Americans to
consistently vote for their party's slate of candidates at all electoral levels.
In other words, are angry voters more likely to vote straight-ticket for
their party's candidates? To answer this question, I re-estimated the model
in Table 6.2 but changed the dependent variable to measure consistent
party loyalty. This variable takes a value of one if the respondent indicated
voting for her party's slate of candidates at the presidential, House,
and Senate levels; all other respondents are coded as zero. The results
of this regression, shown in Table 6.4, are remarkably similar to the
regressions of anger and voter loyalty seen previously. Once again, more

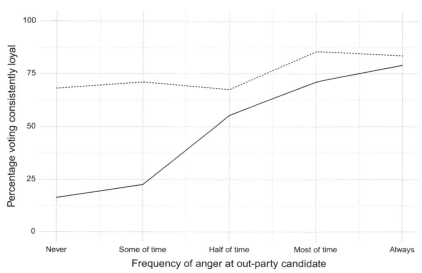

FIGURE 6.5. Anger and consistent voter loyalty. This figure shows the relationship between anger at the opposing party's presidential candidate and voting consistently loyal for one's own party's slate of candidates at the presidential, House, and Senate levels. The relationship between anger and consistent voter loyalty in elections is most pronounced for those individuals who hold negative or neutral views of their own party's presidential candidate.

frequently feeling angry toward the opposing party's presidential candidate is associated with a greater probability that an individual remains loyal at the ballot box. This is true even when controlling for an individual's level of anxiety toward the opposing party's presidential candidate. However, these results build on the previous findings by showing that anger can lead to *consistent* voter loyalty at all levels of the federal electoral system.

As with the previous relationships between anger and voter loyalty, the relationship between anger and consistent voter loyalty is most pronounced for those individuals who hold negative or neutral views of their own party's presidential candidate. This relationship is shown in Figure 6.5. Among those individuals who felt negative or neutral toward their own party's presidential candidate and never felt angry toward the opposing party's presidential candidate, only 16.3% voted consistently loyal for their own party's candidates. Among those individuals who did not like their own party's presidential candidate but reported feeling angry at the opposing party's presidential candidate "half of the time," 55.2% voted consistently loyal for their party's slate of candidates. The percentage voting loyally increased to 71.1% and 79% when respondents who did not like their own party's presidential candidate felt angry at the opposing party's presidential candidate "most of the time" or "always," respectively.

However, unlike the relationships shown in Figures 6.2 and 6.3, anger appears to be associated with a higher likelihood of consistent voter loyalty even when voters already like their own party's presidential candidate. Despite a slight dip in consistent voter loyalty among those individuals who liked their own party's presidential candidate and felt angry at the opposing party's presidential candidate "half of the time," the general trend here is positive. Among this set of respondents, 68% of those who never felt angry at the opposing party's presidential candidate voted consistently loyal for their party's slate of candidates. Among this same group of people, 83.5% of those who reported "always" feeling angry at the opposing party's presidential candidate voted consistently loyal for their own party's candidates. Thus, while the relationship between anger and consistent voter loyalty is more dramatic for those individuals who did not particularly care for their own party's presidential candidate, these results indicate that anger was also associated with consistent voter loyalty for those who *did* like their own party's presidential nominee in 2016.

The results of the models presented in Tables 6.3 and 6.4, along with the trends displayed in Figures 6.3–6.5, suggest that the nationalization of American politics has facilitated a climate in which anger toward the opposing party's presidential candidate is predictive of voting loyally in subpresidential elections. Though the relationship between anger and voter loyalty is weaker in these subpresidential elections than in presidential elections, the fact that anger toward a party's standard-bearer can trickle down to influence voter behavior in other elections is quite impressive.

6.5 JUST POLARIZATION?

One alternative explanation for these findings is that that voters are simply responding to elite-level polarization. As elites become more polarized and offer consistently clear signals about issues and partisan stances (Layman and Carsey 2002), it is possible that voters adopt high levels of loyalty at the ballot box as a result. In other words, it is possible that anger is merely a second-order condition or by-product of polarization, and voters' behavior has been altered due to polarization and not anger.

It is true that, along with voter anger, elite-level polarization has increased considerably over the past three decades. However, this simultaneous increase does not necessarily imply that polarization has caused voter anger. In the abstract, it is possible to imagine a society whose political culture is both polarized and civil. Polarization entails a bimodal distribution of opinions with a high amount of variance (DiMaggio, Evans, and Bryson 1996). Such a definition, which focuses on the "pulling apart" of two distributions, does not require any amount of anger. For example, a country's political elites and citizenry may be divided on the issue of global climate change. Some of the population may favor enacting policies designed to limit the amount of carbon emissions in the air, while others may believe that climate change is not an immediate problem and requires little legislative attention. Whether those individuals who hold these polarized opinions exhibit anger is a separate question. Polarization then, in a theoretical sense, is a plausibly distinct phenomenon from anger.

Such logic is cogently illustrated in work examining the nature of moral convictions in the mass public. When issues take on a moral tone for individuals – for instance, views on abortion among evangelical Christians – research has shown that "interpersonal distance from dissimilar others" increases (Skitka, Bauman, and Sargis 2005). Importantly, this same study found that this interpersonal distance persisted even when factoring in the extremity or intensity of an individual's views.[8] Just as moral convictions and issue extremity and intensity are separate from each other, we can similarly expect polarization and anger to be separate – albeit related – phenomena. And, just as attitudes that are held with a moral conviction have a more pronounced effect on various social outcomes than those attitudes that are merely strongly held, anger should be able to produce voter loyalty independent of polarization.

To more clearly examine the relationship between polarization and anger I utilize a combination of data from the ANES cumulative file and the first dimension of DW-NOMINATE scores.[9] DW-NOMINATE scores rely on roll call votes in Congress to measure the ideological leanings

---

[8] For more on moral convictions, see Greene and Haidt (2002) and Feinberg and Willer (2012).

[9] The data used for this analysis were downloaded from https://legacy.voteview.com/pmediant.htm. Accessed January 28, 2019.

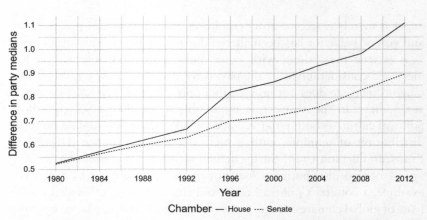

FIGURE 6.6. Polarization in Congress, 1980–2012. This figure shows the distance between the ideology of the median Republican and the ideology of the median Democrat in Congress from 1980 to 2012. The figure indicates that ideological polarization has increased in both the House of Representatives and the Senate.

of each Member of Congress.[10] Accordingly, by aggregating these scores to the chamber-level, it is possible to calculate the amount of political polarization between Democrats and Republicans in both the House of Representatives and the Senate. Greater distances between the two parties indicates a higher degree of polarization. These distances, which I have calculated for each presidential election year between 1980 and 2012 (inclusive), are shown in Figure 6.6.

As shown in Figure 6.6, the distance between the median Republican's ideology and the median Democrat's ideology has increased over time. This is true for both the House of Representatives and the Senate. Does this increase in elite polarization explain rising voter anger? An analysis of the correlation between these increasing levels of polarization and the proportion of voters who reported feeling angry at the opposing party's presidential candidate suggests that the answer is "no." Indeed, the correlation between partisan polarization in the House and voter anger is .38. The correlation between partisan polarization in the Senate and voter anger is a smaller .35. These relatively weak correlations indicate that, while there is a relationship between elite polarization and voter anger, they are distinct phenomena.

[10] DW-NOMINATE scores range from −1, the most liberal score, to 1, the most conservative score.

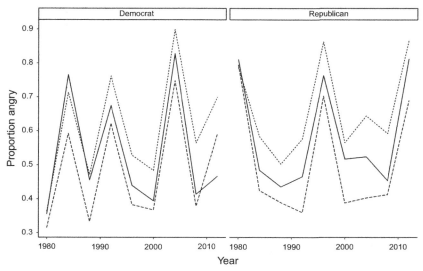

FIGURE 6.7. Anger and strength of partisan identification, 1980–2012. This figure shows the proportion of voters who reported feeling angry at the opposing party's presidential candidate, broken out by strength of partisan identification. The left panel shows the proportion of Democrats who reported feeling angry at the Republican presidential candidate; the right panel shows the proportion of Republicans who reported feeling angry at the Democratic presidential candidate.

Data come from the American National Election Studies cumulative data file.

One additional way to examine the relationship between elite polarization and voter anger is to examine the proportion of voters who ever reported feeling angry at the opposing party's presidential candidate at various levels of partisan strength. To the extent that political elites have increasingly sent polarized and anger-inducing cues over time, it is the most committed partisans who should be most receptive to these cues (Layman and Carsey 2002). Thus, we should expect to see those who identify as "strong partisans" express the highest amount of anger at the opposing party's presidential candidate. This should be followed by more weakly committed partisans and, finally, by those who identify as independents who merely lean toward one of the two major parties. These relationships, measured from 1980 to 2012, are shown graphically in Figure 6.7. The left panel documents the proportion of Democrats who reported feeling angry at the Republican Party's presidential candidate.

The right panel documents the proportion of Republicans who reported feeling angry at the Democratic Party's presidential candidate. The trends displayed in Figure 6.7 indicate that, among both Democrats and Republicans, those who identify as "strong partisans" are the most likely to report feeling angry at the opposing party's presidential candidate. However, rather than more weakly committed partisans, it is actually those individuals who report identifying as independents who lean toward one of the parties that exhibit the second highest amount of anger.

Perhaps more importantly, the nature of these trends provides further evidence that anger and polarization are separate phenomena. Figure 6.6 illustrates that elite polarization has increased monotonically over the past three decades. By contrast, the amount of anger exhibited by partisans has varied across election years: in some years anger is a prominent feature on the political landscape while, in others, partisans are less outraged. The different nature of the trends shown in Figures 6.6 and 6.7 indicates that, rather than being a function of some common underlying feature, polarization and anger are distinct characteristics of American political competition. Thus, while polarization may offer voters more clearly defined choices of candidates, it is anger – rather than political polarization per se – that is the impetus behind the high levels of contemporary voter loyalty described in this chapter.

6.6 CONCLUSION AND DISCUSSION

If anger has harmful consequences for American government, such as reducing political trust and weakening the citizenry's commitment to democratic norms and values, then why do politicians persist in running campaigns that seek to trigger voters' anger? I have sought to answer this pressing question with the preceding analyses. My argument is that politicians continue to run anger-fueled campaigns, even though anger has systemic consequences, because making voters angry is essential to winning votes. Because politicians are first and foremost seeking to win elections (Mayhew 1974), they will employ any objective that aids in this goal – even if it lowers Americans' trust in their own government and reduces the public's commitment to democratic norms and values.

Importantly, the results presented in this chapter indicate that anger's ability to influence voting behavior extends beyond presidential elections. In fact, eliciting anger toward the opposing party's presidential candidate can be beneficial to the electoral fortunes of House and Senate candidates. Such a finding is explained by the growing nationalization of American elections, in which subpresidential electoral competitions are increasingly defined by presidential politics (Abramowitz and Webster 2016; Hopkins 2018). Thus, the incentive for politicians to stoke voter anger extends beyond presidential candidates; in the contemporary era of nationalized politics, even candidates for the House and Senate have valid reasons to encourage their supporters to be angry at the opposing party's standard-bearer.

Two observations about the current state of American politics makes the use of anger as a campaign tactic normatively troubling. First, the fact that politicians' overriding concern with getting elected is unlikely to go away means that the strategic use of anger by candidates is likely to persist. Absent some structural reform that reorganizes the incentives politicians face, the nature of American political discourse is set to remain decisively negative in tone. Second, given the continual growth in negative partisanship and affective polarization within the electorate (Abramowitz and Webster 2016; Iyengar, Sood, and Lelkes 2012), the *degree* to which politicians use anger as a campaign tactic is likely to increase. Indeed, to the extent that political competition is oriented around the parties and candidates that people dislike rather than the ones they like, there is a strong incentive to make the opposing party, its candidates, and its supporters appear as negative as possible by eliciting increasingly strong degrees of anger. Should such anger-inducing rhetoric and strategies lead to the "political dehumanization" (Crawford, Modri, and Motyl 2013) of those who hold different political views, American politics may become irrevocably broken.

Anger and the Future of American Government

Whate'ers begun in anger ends in shame.
— Benjamin Franklin

The preceding analyses in this book have shown that anger plays a broad and powerful role in shaping American public opinion and political behavior. Indeed, the results displayed in previous chapters have shown that anger causes citizens to lose trust in the national government, to weaken in their commitment to democratic norms and values, and to vote increasingly loyal for their own party's slate of candidates for elected office. Each of these consequences of anger has ramifications for the health of American democracy. For instance, because anger is able to lower citizens' trust in government, and because trust in government facilitates support for social welfare programs (Hetherington 2005) and allows for governmental accountability and responsiveness, increases in anger within the mass public are likely to have two effects: first, higher levels of anger are likely to lead to a further erosion in support for programs that seek to make society more egalitarian; and, second, higher levels of anger should cause Americans to increasingly perceive their government to be both unaccountable and unresponsive.

That anger can lower individuals' commitment to democratic norms and values is even more troubling. Absent respect for minority opinions and tolerance for those who hold different opinions, American politics is likely to further transition from a competition of ideas and philosophies to a zero-sum conflict where the stakes are increasingly high and one's political opponents are seen as unworthy of participating. This, too, is likely to further weaken the degree to which the American government is both accountable and responsive to its citizens.

Finally, the preceding chapters in this book have argued that greater levels of anger within the electorate are associated with a higher probability of voting consistently loyal for one's own party. This result is clearly seen at the presidential level; however, with the emergence of a nationalized era of political competition this result now extends to elections for the US House of Representatives and the Senate. If a sign of a healthy democracy is that citizens select good candidates and reject those who are poor in quality (Ferejohn 1986), then the rise in partisan loyalty engendered by anger within the electorate is problematic. Rather than objectively assessing each candidate and choosing the one who is best, Americans today are largely casting votes for their party's candidates regardless of objective quality. The rise of anger within the American electorate has exacerbated the tribal nature of partisanship.

7.1 CAN IT BE REVERSED?

If anger is the cause of these deleterious trends regarding American government and politics, the natural question is whether the growth in anger can be reversed or, absent a reversal, whether this anger can be alleviated. Current trends suggest that anger in the mass public is unlikely to decline. Figure 7.1 plots data from the Pew Research Center showing the percentage of Americans who reported feeling "angry," "frustrated," or "content" with the federal government.[1] A line of best fit is included with each time series to help illustrate the overall trend. When Pew first began asking this question in October 1997, only 12% of respondents reported that they felt angry with the federal government. This percentage declined slightly at the turn of the millennium and in the wake of the September 11, 2001, terrorist attacks. However, by 2006, one in five Americans reported feeling angry with the federal government. Since then, the average percentage of Americans who reported feeling angry with the federal government increased slightly to 22%. Compared to the beginning of the time series, the percentage of Americans who reported feeling angry with the federal government in the last time period in the series had increased by 83%.

---

[1] Those who indicated that they "don't know" how they feel about the federal government are not included.

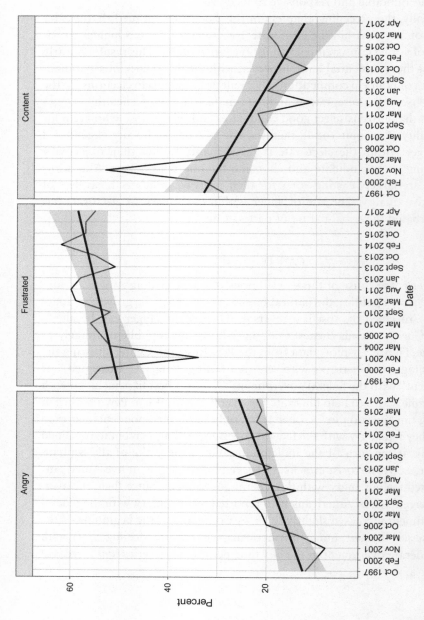

FIGURE 7.1. How Americans feel about their government. This figure shows the percentage of Americans who indicated that they felt "angry," "frustrated," or "content" with the national government.

Data come from the Pew Research Center.

This over time increase in the percentage of Americans who felt angry with the federal government appears to have come at the expense of those who say that they felt "content" with the government. In October 1997, 29% of Americans reported feeling "basically content" with the federal government. This measure reached its nadir (11%) in August 2011 before rebounding in subsequent years. By April 2017, 19% of Americans reported feeling "basically content" with the federal government. This represents a drop of nearly 34% from the first point in the time series to the last in the percentage of Americans who reported feeling content with the federal government.

Meanwhile, the percentage of Americans who reported feeling "frustrated" with the federal government remained comparatively stable over the twenty-year time series. In October 1997, a majority of Americans – 56% – reported that they felt frustrated with the federal government. Absent a sharp drop in the percentage of Americans who reported feeling frustrated with the government after the September 11, 2001, terrorist attacks, this metric has been quite stable over time. In the final time period of the time series, April 2017, 55% of Americans reported feeling frustrated with the federal government – nearly identical to the 56% who expressed this emotion in 1997.

To the extent that the past is prologue, it appears unlikely that anger among the mass public is going to decline. On the contrary, the trends shown in Figure 7.1 – as well as the trends in social media usage – suggest that anger is only going to continue to rise. Indeed, additional data from the Pew Research Center indicates that Americans who are active on Facebook are quite angry with the state of political affairs. According to the Pew report, after February 24, 2016 – when Facebook introduced a new set of possible reactions to posts – Americans increasingly registered angry reactions to politicians' posts. In fact, the new anger option quickly became one of the most used reactions to political posts. By the end of 2017, 11% of political posts elicited angry responses.[2] Taken together, these trends suggest that the over time growth in anger is unlikely to reverse.

If the growth in anger among the mass public is unlikely to reverse, is it possible to alleviate the negative effects of this anger? This, too, appears unlikely. The results presented in the preceding chapters show that anger

---

[2] See the full Pew study at www.pewresearch.org/fact-tank/2018/07/18/anger-topped-love-facebook-after-2016-election/. Accessed September 8, 2018.

causes people to lose trust in the government and to weaken their commitment to democratic norms and values. Importantly, these effects were obtained after a one-time experimental induction of anger. During the course of an individual's daily life, he or she experiences myriad stimuli that arouse anger. This suggests that, rather than alleviating anger, an individual's lived experience – especially among those who are politically attentive – is likely to compound the harmful effects of anger.

Additionally, the anger inductions used here were innocuous compared to the strength of the anger-inducing stimuli that people encounter in their daily lives. In the treatments used throughout this book, individuals were asked to write a short paragraph about a time they were angry. Such an experience is relatively tranquil compared to the events that often transpire in daily life. In the "real world," people get angry about many things: a fight with a friend, a car wreck, the ending of a relationship, or any number of things. Experiencing these events is much more anger-inducing and more emotionally harmful than simply writing about them months or years after they have occurred. Accordingly, not only are people exposed to anger-inducing stimuli more frequently than the one-time manipulations used throughout this book, the stimuli experienced throughout the course of one's life are almost certainly stronger than the ones used in the preceding analyses.

7.2 CONSEQUENCES OF ANGER FOR AMERICAN GOVERNMENT

The trends discussed above indicate that anger in American politics is unlikely to abate. Such an expectation has the potential to powerfully shape the nature of governmental responsiveness in the United States. Powell (2005) argues that responsiveness is best understood as the government doing what its citizens want. The results presented throughout the preceding chapters of this book suggest that politicians today have less of an incentive to do what the citizenry wants and more of an incentive to do only what their copartisans in the electorate want. As long as Americans continue to harbor anger toward the government and the opposing political party and its supporters, political elites will continue to face an incentive structure that prioritizes partisan responsiveness over responsiveness to the entire electorate.

Similarly, the growth of anger within the electorate is likely to change the nature of governmental representation. While previous eras frequently saw bipartisan cooperation in Congress (see, e.g., Mayhew 2001), the anger-fueled nature of contemporary American politics leaves little room for Republicans and Democrats in Congress to work together. Indeed, the results presented throughout this book have shown that Americans are easily made angry. Oftentimes, this anger is a result of frustration with the opposing political party and its supporters. The nature of this anger produces little incentive for politicians to cooperate or work with members of the opposing party. After all, if one's supporters are angry at the out-party, why would a politician want to risk the wrath of his or her supporters by cooperating with an individual who represents policies and people that evoke anger? Doing so is likely to be harmful to a politician's career. Accordingly, the growth in anger within the American electorate has produced an environment in which Democrats and Republicans in Congress are only willing to work with copartisans in terms of advancing legislation. Bipartisanship may be a thing of the past.

Politicians today are able to limit themselves to partisan responsiveness and partisan representation because the prevalence of anger within the electorate has altered the nature of political accountability. Chapter 6 showed how anger is associated with high rates of partisan loyalty at both the presidential and subpresidential levels. With anger continuing to rise, Democrats and Republicans need not worry about their copartisans in the electorate breaking ranks and casting a vote for a candidate from the opposing party. This high rate of partisan loyalty in voting, combined with the increasing number of districts that have a clear partisan lean, indicates that Members of Congress are largely accountable only to their partisan base in the electorate.

Paradoxically, the ways in which anger has changed governmental responsiveness, representation, and accountability are likely to further perpetuate the amount of anger within the American electorate. As politicians become increasingly concerned with responding to and representing their copartisans in the electorate at the expense of their entire constituency, those constituents who do not belong to the politician's party are likely to grow ever more angry by their lack of voice in Congress. This anger is almost certainly going to be directed at the opposing political party. This anger, in turn, will serve to further exacerbate the perverse forms of responsiveness and representation described above. In sum, the growth of anger within the electorate and the partisan nature of responsiveness and representation among political elites are mutually reinforcing phenomena.

In addition to the feedback loop between voter anger and subpar governmental responsiveness, representation, and accountability, it is also likely that anger within the electorate, diminishing trust in government, and a weakening commitment to democratic norms and values are reinforcing phenomena. Chapters 3 and 4 argued that higher levels of anger, whether conceptualized as a personality trait or an emotion, serve to lower one's trust in the national government. The evidence presented in Chapter 5 suggests that anger does more than just lower trust in government; indeed, higher amounts of anger can actually cause citizens to adopt opinions that are antithetical to a properly functioning democratic society. When individuals have little trust in the national government and possess opinions and attitudes about the political opposition that run counter to the democratic ideal, anger – at the government, those who run it, and supporters of the opposing party – is likely to increase. This anger only further exacerbates the growing distrust Americans have in their government and their lack of tolerance for those with whom they disagree politically.

Taken as a whole, the results in this book present a worrying outlook for the health of American democracy. Anger lowers citizens' trust in the national government and weakens their commitment to democratic norms and values. Moreover, it is likely that these are mutually reinforcing phenomena. Finding a way to remove the heightened levels of anger that are present in our political discourse would help to remedy these societal ills; however, because politicians are primarily concerned with being re-elected and because anger aids in this pursuit, hoping for an elite-driven abatement of this angry style of politics is unlikely to bear fruit. Absent some major event that reorients the incentive structures facing both political elites and citizens, anger is likely to persist as an overarching theme of American politics. We have reason to be worried.

Bibliography

Abramowitz, Alan I. 2010. *The Disappearing Center: Engaged Citizens, Polarization, and American Democracy.* Yale University Press.

Abramowitz, Alan I. and Kyle L. Saunders. 1998. "Ideological Realignment in the U.S. Electorate." *The Journal of Politics* 60(3):634–652.

Abramowitz, Alan I. and Steven W. Webster. 2016. "The Rise of Negative Partisanship and the Nationalization of U.S. Elections in the 21st Century." *Electoral Studies* 41:12–22.

Abramowitz, Alan I. and Steven W. Webster. 2018a. The Angry American Voter: Negative Partisanship, Voter Anger, and the 2016 Presidential Election. In *State of the Parties*, ed. John C. Green, Daniel J. Coffey, and David B. Cohen. University of Akron Press, pp. 185–197.

Abramowitz, Alan I. and Steven W. Webster. 2018b. "Negative Partisanship: Why Americans Dislike Parties But Behave Like Rabid Partisans." *Political Psychology* 39:119–135.

Abrams, Abigail. 2019. "Robert Mueller's Legacy Will Haunt Donald Trump." https://time.com/5598470/robert-mueller-investigation-haunt-donald-trump/. Accessed: 2019-09-22.

Acemoglu, Daron and James A. Robinson. 2006. *Economic Origins of Dictatorship and Democracy.* Cambridge University Press.

Adorno, Theodor W., Else Frenkel-Brunswik, Daniel Levinson, and Nevitt Sanford. 1950. *The Authoritarian Personality.* Harper and Brothers.

Albertson, Bethany and Shana Kushner Gadarian. 2015. *Anxious Politics: Democratic Citizenship in a Threatening World.* Cambridge University Press.

Allen, Bem P. 1994. *Personality Theories.* Allyn and Bacon.

Allport, Gordon W. 1954. *The Nature of Prejudice.* Beacon Press.

Allport, Gordon W. and Henry S. Odbert. 1936. "Trait-Names: A Psycho-Lexical Study." *Psychological Monographs* 47(1):1–171.

Allred, Keith G. 1999. Anger and Retaliation: Toward an Understanding of Impassioned Conflict in Organizations. In *Research on Negotiation in Organizations*, ed. Robert J. Bies, Roy J. Lewicki, and Blair H. Sheppard. JAI Press, pp. 27–58.

Allred, Keith G., John S. Mallozzi, Fusako Matsui, and Christopher P. Raia. 1997. "The Influence of Anger and Compassion on Negotiation Performance." *Organizational Behavior and Human Decision Processes* 70(3):175–187.

Anderson, Christopher J., Andrè Blais, Shaun Bowler, Todd Donovan, and Ola Listhaug. 2005. *Losers' Consent: Elections and Democratic Legitimacy.* Oxford University Press.

Arceneaux, Kevin and Martin Johnson. 2013. *Changing Minds or Changing Channels?: Partisan News in an Age of Choice.* University of Chicago Press.

Averill, James R. 1982. *Anger and Aggression: An Essay on Emotion.* Springer-Verlag.

Bafumi, Joseph and Robert Y. Shapiro. 2009. "A New Partisan Voter." *Journal of Politics* 71(1):1–24.

Bakshy, Eytan, Solomon Messing, and Lada A. Adamic. 2015. "Exposure to Ideologically Diverse News and Opinion on Facebook." *Science* 348(6239):1130–1132.

Banda, Kevin K. and John Cluverius. 2018. "Elite Polarization, Party Extremity, and Affective Polarization." *Electoral Studies* 56:90–101.

Banks, Antoine J. 2014. "The Public's Anger: White Racial Attitudes and Opinions toward Health Care Reform." *Political Behavior* 36:493–514.

Banks, Antoine J. and Nicholas A. Valentino. 2012. "Emotional Substrates of White Racial Attitudes." *American Journal of Political Science* 56(2):286–297.

Bennett, Roger. 1997. "Anger, Catharsis, and Purchasing Behavior Following Aggressive Customer Complaints." *Journal of Consumer Marketing* 14(2):156–172.

Binder, Sarah A. 1999. "The Dynamics of Legislative Gridlock, 1947-1996." *American Political Science Review* 93(3):519–533.

Binder, Sarah A. 2004. *Stalemate: Causes and Consequences of Legislative Gridlock.* Brookings Institution Press.

Black, Earl and Merle Black. 2002. *The Rise of Southern Republicans.* Harvard University Press.

Bodenhausen, Galen V., Lori A. Sheppard, and Geoffrey P. Kramer. 1994. "Negative Affect and Social Judgment: The Differential Impact of Anger and Sadness." *European Journal of Social Psychology* 24(1):45–62.

Bollen, Kenneth A. 1980. "Issues in the Comparative Measurement of Political Democracy." *American Sociological Review* 45(3):370–390.

Bollen, Kenneth A. 1993. "Liberal Democracy: Validity and Method Factors in Cross-National Measures." *American Journal of Political Science* 37(4):1207–1230.

Bollen, Kenneth A. and Pamela Paxton. 2000. "Subjective Measures of Liberal Democracy." *Comparative Political Studies* 33(1):58–86.

Bower, Gordon H. 1991. Mood Congruity of Social Judgments. In *Emotions and Social Judgments,* ed. Joseph P. Forgas. Pergamon Press, pp. 31–53.

Brader, Ted, Nicholas A. Valentino, and Elizabeth Suhay. 2008. "What Triggers Public Opposition to Immigration? Anxiety, Group Cues, and Immigration Threat." *American Journal of Political Science* 52(4):959–978.

Bratton, Michael and Nicolas van de Walle. 1997. *Democratic Experiments in Africa: Regime Transitions in Comparative Perspective*. Cambridge University Press.

Buss, David M. 1999. Human Nature and Individual Differences: The Evolution of Human Personality. In *Handbook of Personality: Theory and Research*, ed. Lawrence A. Pervin and Oliver P. John. The Guilford Press, pp. 31–56.

Campbell, Angus, Philip E. Converse, Warren E. Miller, and Donald E. Stokes. 1960. *The American Voter*. Wiley.

Chernow, Ron. 2005. *Alexander Hamilton*. Penguin Books.

Citrin, Jack. 1974. "Comment: The Political Relevance of Trust in Government." *American Political Science Review* 68(3):973–988.

Cobb-Clark, Deborah A. and Stefanie Schurer. 2012. "The Stability of Big-Five Personality Traits." *Economics Letters* 115:11–15.

Collins, Eliza. 2016. "Poll: Clinton, Trump Most Unfavorable Candidates Ever." www.usatoday.com/story/news/politics/onpolitics/2016/08/31/poll-clinton-trump-most-unfavorable-candidates-ever/89644296/. Accessed: 2018-04-26.

Conley, Timothy G., Christian B. Hansen, and Peter E. Rossi. 2008. "Plausibly Exogenous." www.princeton.edu/ erp/erp%20seminar%20pdfs/papers spring09/Rossi%20paper%202.pdf. Accessed: 2018-10-06.

Cooper, Christopher A., Lauren Golden, and Alan Socha. 2013. "The Big Five Personality Factors and Mass Politics." *Journal of Applied Social Psychology* 43(1):68–82.

Coppock, Alexander and Oliver A. McClellan. 2018. "Validating the Demographic, Political, Psychological, and Experimental Results Obtained from a New Source of Online Survey Respondents." *Research & Politics*. DOI: 10.1177/2053168018822174.

Costa, Paul T. and Robert R. McCrae. 1995. "Domains and Facets: Personality Assessment Using the Revised NEO Personality Inventory." *Journal of Personality Assessment* 64(1):21–50.

Cox, Gary W. and Matthew D. McCubbins. 2005. *Setting the Agenda: Responsible Party Government in the U.S. House of Representatives*. Cambridge University Press.

Craig, Maureen A. and Jennifer A. Richeson. 2017. "Information about the U.S. Racial Demographic Shift Triggers Concerns about Anti-White Discrimination among the Prospective White 'Minority'." *PLoS ONE* 12(9). DOI: 10.1371/journal.pone.0185389.

Crawford, Jarret T., Sean A. Modri, and Matt Motyl. 2013. "Bleeding-Heart Liberals and Hard-Hearted Conservatives: Subtle Political Dehumanization through Differential Attributions of Human Nature and Human Uniqueness Traits." *Journal of Social and Political Psychology* 1:86–104.

Dahl, Robert A. 1971. *Polyarchy: Participation and Opposition*. Yale University Press.

DeBenedetti, Charles. 1990. *An American Ordeal: The Antiwar Movement of the Vietnam Era*. Stanford University Press.

DellaVigna, Stefano and Ethan Kaplan. 2007. "The Fox News Effect: Media Bias and Voting." *The Quarterly Journal of Economics* 122(3):1187–1234.

Digman, John M. 1989. "Five Robust Trait Dimensions: Development, Stability, and Utility." *Journal of Personality* 57(2):195–214.

DiMaggio, Paul, John Evans, and Bethany Bryson. 1996. "Have Americans' Social Attitudes Become More Polarized?" *American Journal of Sociology* 102(3):690–755.

Downs, Anthony. 1957. *An Economic Theory of Democracy*. Harper.

Dunn, Jennifer R. and Maurice E. Schweitzer. 2005. "Feeling and Believing: The Influence of Emotion on Trust." *Journal of Personality and Social Psychology* 88(5):736–748.

Dunwoody, Philip T. and Sam G. McFarland. 2017. "Support for Anti-Muslim Policies: The Role of Political Traits and Threat Perception." *Political Psychology* 39(1):89–106.

Dvir-Gvirsman, Shira. 2016. "Media Audience Homophily: Partisan Websites, Audience Identity and Polarization Processes." *New Media & Society* 19(7):1072–1091.

Feinberg, Matthew and Robb Willer. 2012. "The Moral Roots of Environmental Attitudes." *Psychological Science* 24(1):56–62.

Feldman, Stanley. 2003. "Enforcing Social Conformity: A Theory of Authoritarianism." *Political Psychology* 24(1):41–74.

Fenno, Richard F. 1978. *Home Style: House Members in Their Districts*. Pearson College Division.

Ferejohn, John. 1986. "Incumbent Performance and Electoral Control." *Public Choice* 50(1):5–25.

Flint, Joe and Rebecca Ballhaus. 2015. "Cable TV News Binges on Trump Coverage." www.wsj.com/articles/cable-tv-news-binges-on-trump-coverage-1442360415?cb=logged0.7896779139991 85. Accessed: 2018-08-22.

Forgas, Joseph P. and Stephanie Moylan. 1987. "After the Movies: Transient Mood and Social Judgments." *Personality and Social Psychology Bulletin* 13(4):467–477.

Fournier, Ron. 2015. "Why We're Voting for the Wrong Reasons." www.theatlantic.com/politics/archive/2015/05/why-were-voting-for-the-wrong-reasons/460842/. Accessed: 2018-01-22.

Frazin, Rachel. 2019. "'Lock her up' Chant Breaks Out at Trump Rally." https://thehill.com/homenews/campaign/455874-lock-her-up-chant-breaks-out-at-trump-rally. Accessed: 2019-09-23.

Frimer, Jeremy A., Mark J. Brandt, Zachary Melton, and Matt Moty. N.d. "Extremists on the Left and Right Use Angry, Negative Language." Working Paper. Available at https://osf.io/5mvyk/. Accessed: 2018-10-19.

Gerber, Alan S., Gregory A. Huber, David Doherty, Conor M. Dowling, and Shang E. Ha. 2010. "Personality and Political Attitudes: Relationships across Issue Domains and Political Contexts." *American Political Science Review* 104(1):111–133.

Gerber, Alan S., Gregory A. Huber, David Doherty, and Conor M. Dowling. 2012. "Disagreement and the Avoidance of Political Discussion: Aggregate Relationships and Differences across Personality Traits." *American Journal of Political Science* 56(4):849–874.

Gervais, Bryan T. 2016. "More Than Mimicry? The Role of Anger in Uncivil Reactions to Elite Political Incivility." *International Journal of Public Opinion Research* 29(3):384–405.

Gilberstadt, Hannah. 2019. "For the First Time, Majority of Republicans Express Confidence in the Fairness of Mueller's Investigation." www.pewresearch.org/fact-tank/2019/07/23/majority-republicans-express-confidence-fairness-mueller-investigation/. Accessed: 2019-09-23.

Gino, Francesca and Maurice E. Schweitzer. 2008. "Blinded by Anger or Feeling the Love: How Emotions Influence Advice Taking." *Journal of Applied Psychology* 93(5):1165–1173.

Glasser, Susan N. 2019. "Trump's Wacky, Angry, and Extreme August." www.newyorker.com/news/letter-from-trumps-washington/trumps-wacky-angry-and-extreme-august-twitter. Accessed: 2019-09-23.

Goldberg, Lewis R., John A. Johnson, Herbert W. Eber, Robert Hogan, Michael C. Ashton, C. Robert Cloninger, and Harrison G. Gough. 2006. "The International Personality Item Pool and the Future of Public-Domain Personality Measures." *Journal of Research in Personality* 40:84–96.

Gorsuch, Richard L. 1983. *Factor Analysis*. 2nd ed. Lawrence Erlbaum Associates.

Gottfried, Jeffrey, Galen Stocking, and Elizabeth Grieco. 2018. "Partisans Remain Sharply Divided in Their Attitudes about the News Media." www.journalism.org/2018/09/25/partisans-remain-sharply-divided-in-their-attitudes-about-the-news-media/. Accessed: 2019-09-23.

Green, Donald, Bradley Palmquist, and Eric Schickler. 2002. *Partisan Hearts and Minds*. Yale University Press.

Greene, Joshua and Jonathan Haidt. 2002. "How (And Where) Does Moral Judgment Work?" *Trends in Cognitive Sciences* 6(12):517–523.

Grimmer, Justin. 2013. *Representational Style in Congress: What Legislators Say and Why It Matters*. Cambridge University Press.

Grimmer, Justin and Gary King. 2011. "General Purpose Computer-Assisted Clustering and Conceptualization." *Proceedings of the National Academy of Sciences* 108(7):2643–2650.

Grossmann, Matt and Daniel Thaler. 2018. "Mass-Elite Divides in Aversion to Social Change and Support for Donald Trump." *American Politics Research* 46(5):753–784.

Guess, Andrew, Brendan Nyhan, and Jason Reifler. 2018. "Selective Exposure to Misinformation: Evidence from the Consumption of Fake News during the 2016 U.S. Presidential Campaign." Working Paper. Available at www.dartmouth.edu/~nyhan/fake-news-2016.pdf.

Hannah-Jones, Nikole. 2019. "It Was Never About Busing." www.nytimes.com/2019/07/12/opinion/sunday/it-was-never-about-busing.html?smtyp=cur&smid=tw-nytopinion. Accessed: 2019-07-14.

Helmke, Gretchen and Steven Levitsky. 2006. *Informal Institutions and Democracy: Lessons from Latin America*. Johns Hopkins University Press.

Hetherington, Marc J. 2005. *Why Trust Matters: Declining Political Trust and the Demise of American Liberalism*. Princeton University Press.

Hetherington, Marc J. and Thomas J. Rudolph. 2015. *Why Washington Won't Work: Polarization, Political Trust, and the Governing Crisis.* University of Chicago Press.

Hetherington, Marc J. and Elizabeth Suhay. 2011. "Authoritarianism, Threat, and Americans' Support for the War on Terror." *American Journal of Political Science* 55(3):546–560.

Hetherington, Marc J. and Jonathan D. Weiler. 2009. *Authoritarianism and Polarization in American Politics.* Cambridge University Press.

Holbert, R. Lance and Glenn J. Hansen. 2008. "Stepping beyond Message Specificity in the Study of Emotion as Mediator and Inter-Emotion Associations across Attitude Objects: Fahrenheit 9/11, Anger, and Debate Euperiority." *Media Psychology* 11(1):98–118.

Hood, M. V., Quentin Kidd, and Irwin L. Morris. 2004. "The Reintroduction of the Elephas Maximus to the Southern United States: The Rise of Republican State Parties, 1960 to 2000." *American Politics Research* 32(1):68–101.

Hopkins, Daniel J. 2018. *The Increasingly United States: How and Why American Political Behavior Nationalized.* University of Chicago Press.

Huddy, Leonie, Lilliana Mason, and Lene Aarøe. 2015. "Expressive Partisanship: Campaign Involvement, Political Emotion, and Partisan Identity." *American Political Science Review* 109(1):1–17.

Iyengar, Shanto and Kyu S. Hahn. 2009. "Red Media, Blue Media: Evidence of Ideological Selectivity in Media Use." *Journal of Communication* 59(1): 19–39.

Iyengar, Shanto and Sean J. Westwood. 2015. "Fear and Loathing across Party Lines: New Evidence on Group Polarization." *American Journal of Political Science* 59(3):690–707.

Iyengar, Shanto, Gaurav Sood, and Yphtach Lelkes. 2012. "Affect, Not Ideology: A Social Identity Perspective on Polarization." *Public Opinion Quarterly* 76(3):405–431.

Jacobson, Gary C. 2015. "It's Nothing Personal: The Decline of the Incumbency Advantage in US House Elections." *The Journal of Politics* 77(3):861–873.

James, William. 1884. "What Is an Emotion?" *Mind* (34):188–205.

Johnston, Christopher D., Christopher M. Federico, and Howard Lavine. 2017. *Open versus Closed: Personality, Identity, and the Politics of Redistribution.* Cambridge University Press.

Jones, Robert P. 2016. *The End of White Christian America.* Simon and Schuster.

Kalmoe, Nathan P. 2018. "Legitimizing Partisan Violence: Evidence of Political Bias in State Violence Views from Four Experiments." Working Paper. Available at www.dropbox.com/s/olwz6jso16rgoip/Kalmoe%20-%20Legitimizing %20Partisan%20Violence.pdf?dl=0.

Keltner, Dacher, Phoebe C. Ellsworth, and Kari Edwards. 1993. "Beyond Simple Pessimism: Effects of Sadness and Anger on Social Perception." *Journal of Personality and Social Psychology* 64(5):740–752.

Kim, Hyo J. and Glen T. Cameron. 2011. "Emotions Matter in Crisis: The Role of Anger and Sadness in the Publics' Response to Crisis News Framing and Corporate Crisis Response." *Communication Research* 38(6):826–855.

Klar, Samara. 2014. "Partisanship in a Social Setting." *American Journal of Political Science* 58(3):687–704.

Klar, Samara and Yanna Krupnikov. 2016. *Independent Politics: How American Disdain for Parties Leads to Political Inaction.* Cambridge University Press.

Krehbiel, Keith. 1998. *Pivotal Politics: A Theory of US Lawmaking.* University of Chicago Press.

Krieg, Gregory. 2016. "Clinton Takes on Trump: Her 34 Toughest Lines." www.cnn.com/2016/06/02/politics/hillary-clinton-attack-lines-donald-trump-foreign-policy/index.html. Accessed: 2018-04-27.

Lapinski, John, Matt Levendusky, Ken Winneg, and Kathleen Hall Jamieson. 2016. "What Do Citizens Want from Their Member of Congress?" *Political Research Quarterly* 69(3):535–545.

Lauth, Hans-Joachim. 2000. "Informal Institutions and Democracy." *Democratization* 7(4):21–50.

Lawrence, Regina G., Logan Molyneux, Mark Coddington, and Avery Holton. 2014. "Tweeting Conventions: Political Journalists' Use of Twitter to Cover the 2012 Presidential Campaign." *Journalism Studies* 14(6):789–806.

Layman, Geoffrey C. and Thomas M. Carsey. 2002. "Party Polarization and 'Conflict Extension' in the American Electorate." *American Journal of Political Science* 46(4):786–802.

Lazarus, Richard S. and Craig A. Smith. 1988. "Knowledge and Appraisal in the Cognition-Emotion Relationship." *Cognition & Emotion* 2(4):281–300.

LeDoux, Joseph. 1998. *The Emotional Brain: The Mysterious Underpinnings of Emotional Life.* Simon and Schuster.

Lee, M. J. and Dan Merica. 2016. "Clinton's Last Campaign Speech: 'Love trumps hate'." www.cnn.com/2016/11/07/politics/hillary-clinton-campaign-final-day/index.html. Accessed: 2018-04-27.

Lerner, Jennifer S. and Dacher Keltner. 2001. "Fear, Anger, and Risk." *Journal of Personality and Social Psychology* 81(1):146–159.

Lerner, Jennifer S. and Larissa Z. Tiedens. 2006. "Portrait of the Angry Decision Maker: How Appraisal Tendencies Shape Anger's Influence on Cognition." *Journal of Behavioral Decision Making* 19:115–137.

Lerner, Jennifer S., Roxana M. Gonzalez, Deborah A. Small, and Baruch Fischhoff. 2003. "Effects of Fear and Anger on Perceived Risks of Terrorism: A National Field Experiment." *Psychological Science* 14(2):144–150.

Levendusky, Matthew S. 2009. *The Partisan Sort: How Liberals Became Democrats and Conservatives Became Republicans.* University of Chicago Press.

Levendusky, Matthew S. 2013. *How Partisan Media Polarize America.* University of Chicago Press.

Levitsky, Steven and Daniel Ziblatt. 2018. *How Democracies Die.* Penguin Random House.

Lijphart, Arend. 1977. *Democracy in Plural Societies: A Comparative Exploration.* Yale University Press.

Lijphart, Arend. 1999. *Patterns of Democracy: Government Forms and Performance in Thirty-Six Countries.* Yale University Press.

Linz, Juan J. and Alfred Stepan. 1996. *Problems of Democratic Transition and Consolidation: Southern Europe, South America, and Post-Communist Europe*. Johns Hopkins University Press.

Lipset, Seymour Martin. 1963. *Political Man: The Social Bases of Politics*. Johns Hopkins University Press.

Lobbestael, Jill, Arnoud Arntz, and Reinout W. Wiers. 2008. "How to Push Someone's Buttons: A Comparison of Four Anger-Induction Methods." *Cognition & Emotion* 22(2):353–373.

Lord, Wendy. 2007. *NEO-PI-R: A Guide to Interpretation and Feedback in a Work Context*. Hogrefe Ltd.

MacKuen, Michael, Jennifer Wolak, Luke Keele, and George E. Marcus. 2010. "Civic Engagements: Resolute Partisanship or Reflective Deliberation." *American Journal of Political Science* 54(2):440–458.

Malka, Ariel and Yphtach Lelkes. 2010. "More Than Ideology: Conservative-Liberal Identity and Receptivity to Political Cues." *Social Justice Research* 23(2–3):156–188.

Marcus, George E. 2002. *The Sentimental Citizen: Emotion in Democratic Politics*. Penn State University Press.

Marcus, George E., W. Russell Neuman, and Michael MacKuen. 2000. *Affective Intelligence and Political Judgment*. University of Chicago Press.

Martin, Gregory J. and Josh McCrain. 2019. "Local News and National Politics." *American Political Science Review* 113 (2): 372–384.

Martin, Gregory J. and Ali Yurukoglu. 2017. "Bias in Cable News: Persuasion and Polarization." *American Economic Review* 107(9):2565–2599.

Mason, Lilliana. 2013. "The Rise of Uncivil Agreement: Issue versus Behavioral Polarization in the American Electorate." *American Behavioral Scientist* 57(1):140–159.

Mason, Lilliana. 2015. "'I Disrespectfully Agree': The Differential Effects of Partisan Sorting on Social and Issue Polarization." *American Journal of Political Science* 59(1):128–145.

Mayhew, David R. 1974. *Congress: The Electoral Connection*. Yale University Press.

Mayhew, David R. 2001. *Divided We Govern: Party Control, Lawmaking, and Investigations, 1946-2002*. Yale University Press.

McCrae, Robert R. and Paul T. Costa. 1994. "The Stability of Personality: Observations and Evaluations." *Current Directions in Psychological Science* 3(6): 173–175.

McGregor, Shannon C. and Logan Molyneux. 2018. "Twitter's Influence on News Judgment: An Experiment among Journalists." *Journalism*. DOI: 10.1177/1464884918802975.

Mondak, Jeffery J. 2010. *Personality and the Foundations of Political Behavior*. Cambridge University Press.

Mondak, Jeffery J. and Karen D. Halperin. 2008. "A Framework for the Study of Personality and Political Behaviour." *British Journal of Political Science* 38(2):335–362.

Mondak, Jeffrey K., Damarys Canache, Mitchell A. Seligson, and Mary R. Anderson. 2010. "Personality and Civic Engagement: An Integrative Framework for the Study of Trait Effects on Political Behavior." *American Political Science Review* 104(1):85–110.

Moons, Wesley G., Naomi I. Eisenberger, and Shelley E. Taylor. 2010. "Anger and Fear Responses to Stress Have Different Biological Profiles." *Brain, Behavior, and Immunity* 24:215–219.

Mourão, Rachel Reis. 2014. "The Boys on the Timeline: Political Journalists' Use of Twitter for Building Interpretive Communities." *Journalism* 16(8): 1107–1123.

Mutz, Diana. 2015. *In-Your-Face Politics: The Consequences of Uncivil Media.* Princeton University Press.

Newhagen, John E. 1998. "TV News Images That Induce Anger, Fear, and Disgust: Effects on Approach-Avoidance and Memory." *Journal of Broadcasting & Electronic Media* 42(2):265–276.

Norris, Pippa. 2008. *Driving Democracy: Do Power-Sharing Institutions Work?* Cambridge University Press.

Pariser, Eli. 2011. *The Filter Bubble: How the New Personalized Web Is Changing What We Read and How We Think.* Penguin.

Paunonen, Sampo V. and Michael C. Ashton. 2001. "Big Five Factors and Facets and the Prediction of Behavior." *Journal of Personality and Social Psychology* 81(3):524–539.

PBS. 2016. "Election 2016 in One Word." www.pbs.org/weta/washingtonweek/web-video/election-2016-one-word. Accessed: 2018-05-11.

Pew Research Center. 2015. "Beyond Distrust: How Americans View Their Government." www.people-press.org/2015/11/23/1-trust-in-government-1958-2015/. Accessed: 2017-01-25.

Piedmont, Ralph L. 1989. *The Revised NEO Personality Inventory: Clinical and Research Applications.* Plenum Press.

Powell, G. Bingham. 2005. The Chain of Responsiveness. In *Assessing the Quality of Democracy*, ed. Larry Diamond and Leonardo Morlino. Johns Hopkins University Press, pp. 61–76.

Prior, Markus. 2007. *Post-Broadcast Democracy: How Media Choice Increases Inequality in Political Involvement and Polarizes Elections.* Cambridge University Press.

Przeworski, Adam. 1991. *Democracy and the Market.* Cambridge University Press.

Reynolds, Sarah K. and Lee Anna Clark. 2001. "Predicting Dimensions of Personality Disorder from Domains and Facets of the Five-Factor Model." *Journal of Personality* 62(2):199–222.

Rhodes, Jesse H. and Amber B. Vayo. 2018. "Fear and Loathing in Presidential Candidate Rhetoric, 1952-2016." Working Paper. Available at www.dropbox.com/s/ec4nwkdgnjlbood/rhodes-vayo-APSA-2018.pdf?dl=0.

Rogowski, Jon C. and Joseph L. Sutherland. 2015. "How Ideology Fuels Affective Polarization." *Political Behavior* 38:1–24.

Roseman, Ira J., Martin S. Spindel, and Paul E. Jose. 1990. "Appraisals of Emotion-Eliciting Events: Testing a Theory of Discrete Emotions." *Journal of Personality and Social Psychology* 59(5):899–915.

Rosenfeld, Sam. 2018. *The Polarizers: Postwar Architects of Our Partisan Era.* University of Chicago Press.

Rubin, Lillian B. 1972. *Busing and Backlash: White against White in a California School District.* University of California Press.

Saad, Lydia. 2016. "Trump and Clinton Finish with Historically Poor Images." http://news.gallup.com/poll/197231/trump-clinton-finish-historically-poor-images.aspx. Accessed: 2018-04-26.

Schwarz, Norbert and Gerald Clore. 1983. "Mood, Misattribution, and Judgments of Well-Being: Informative and Directive Functions of Affective States." *Journal of Personality and Social Psychology* 45(3):513–523.

Silvia, Paul J. 2009. "Looking Past Pleasure: Anger, Confusion, Disgust, Pride, Surprise, and Other Unusual Aesthetic Emotions." *Psychology of Aesthetics, Creativity, and the Arts* 3(1):48–51.

Sinclair, Barbara. 1997. *Unorthodox Lawmaking: New Legislative Processes in the U.S. Congress.* CQ Press.

Skitka, Linda J., Christopher W. Bauman, and Edward G. Sargis. 2005. "Moral Conviction: Another Contributor to Attitude Strength or Something More?" *Journal of Personality and Social Psychology* 88(6):895–917.

Skocpol, Theda and Vanessa Williamson. 2016. *The Tea Party and the Remaking of Republican Conservatism.* Oxford University Press.

Smith, Gregory A. and Jessica Martinez. 2016. "How the Faithful Voted: A Preliminary 2016 Analysis." www.pewresearch.org/fact-tank/2016/11/09/how-the-faithful-voted-a-preliminary-2016-analysis/. Accessed: 2019-02-11.

Smith, Samantha. 2016. "6 Charts That Show Where Clinton and Trump Supporters Differ." www.pewresearch.org/fact-tank/2016/10/20/6-charts-that-show-where-clinton-and-trump-supporters-differ/. Accessed: 2019-01-12.

Sood, Gaurav and Shanto Iyengar. 2018. "All in the Eye of the Beholder: Partisan Affect and Ideological Accountability." In *The Feeling, Thinking Citizen: Essays in Honor of Milton Lodge*, ed. Howard Lavine and Charles S. Taber. Routledge, pp. 195–228

Sunstein, Cass R. 2001. *Republic.com.* Princeton University Press.

Svolik, Milan W. 2018. "When Polarization Trumps Civic Virtue: Partisan Conflict and the Subversion of Democracy by Incumbents." Working Paper. Available at https://cpb-us-w2.wpmucdn.com/campuspress.yale.edu/dist/6/1038/files/2017/11/Svolik-Polarization-16xwfa7.pdf.

Taub, Amanda and Max Fisher. 2017. "As Leaks Multiply, Fears of a 'Deep State' in America." www.nytimes.com/2017/02/16/world/americas/deep-state-leaks-trump.html?_r=0&referer=https://t.co/WwEWvgjncz. Accessed: 2019-09-23.

Tauszcik, Yla R. and James W. Pennebaker. 2010. "The Psychological Meaning of Words: LIWC and Computerized Text Analysis Methods." *Journal of Language of Social Psychology* 29(1):24–54.

The Economist. 2017. "Declining Trust in Government Is Denting Democracy." www.economist.com/blogs/graphicdetail/2017/01/daily-chart-20?fsrc=scn/tw/te/bl/ed/decliningtrustingovernmentisdentingdemocracy. Accessed: 2017-01-25.

Tiedens, Larissa Z. 2001. "The Effect of Anger on the Hostile Inferences of Aggressive and Nonaggressive People: Specific Emotions, Cognitive Processing, and Chronic Accessibility." *Motivation and Emotion* 25(3):233–251.

Tocqueville, Alexis de. 1835. *Democracy in America.*

Valentino, Nicholas A., Krysha Gregorowicz, and Eric W. Groenendyk. 2009. "Efficacy, Emotions and the Habit of Participation." *Political Behavior* 31(3):307–330.

Valentino, Nicholas A., Ted Brader, Eric W. Groenendyk, Krysha Gregorowicz, and Vincent L. Hutchings. 2011. "Election Night's Alright for Fighting: The Role of Emotions in Political Participation." *The Journal of Politics* (1):156–170.

Wagner, Michael W. and Mike Gruszczynski. 2017. "Who Gets Covered? Ideological Extremity and News Coverage of Members of the U.S. Congress, 1993 to 2013." *Journalism & Mass Communication Quarterly* 95(3):670–690.

Webb, Daryl. 1995. "Crusade: George McGovern's Opposition to the Vietnam War." Master's Thesis, St. Cloud State University.

Webster, Steven W. 2018a. "Anger and Declining Trust in Government in the American Electorate." *Political Behavior* 40(4): 933–964.

Webster, Steven W. 2018b. "It's Personal: The Big Five Personality Traits and Negative Partisan Affect in Polarized U.S. Politics." *American Behavioral Scientist* 62(1):127–145.

Webster, Steven W. and Alan I. Abramowitz. 2017. "The Ideological Foundations of Affective Polarization in the US Electorate." *American Politics Research* 45(4):621–647.

Weiner, Bernard. 2000. "Intrapersonal and Interpersonal Theories of Motivation from an Attributional Perspective." *Educational Psychology Review* 12: 1–14.

Wells, Tom. 1994. *The War Within: America's Battle over Vietnam.* University of California Press.

Wiggins, Jerry S. 1996. *The Five-Factor Model of Personality: Theoretical Perspectives.* Guilford Press.

Williamson, Vanessa, Theda Skocpol, and John Coggin. 2011. "The Tea Party and the Remaking of Republican Conservatism." *Perspectives on Politics* 9(1): 25–43.

Zahn, Harry. 2016. "Why 'Negative Partisanship' Is Flipping Politics on Its Head." www.pbs.org/newshour/politics/negative-partisanship-flipping-politics-head. Accessed: 2018-01-22.

Index

Made in the USA
Middletown, DE
04 September 2024

60316090R00113